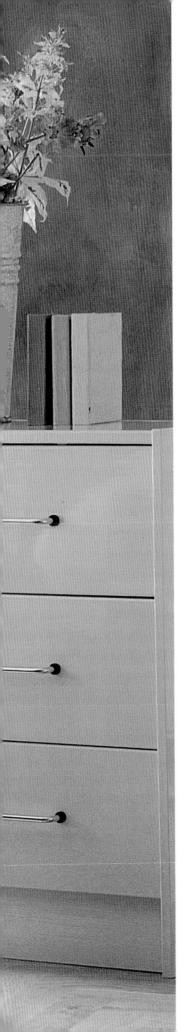

FURNITURE
FACELIFTS

Liz Wagstaff

with Mark Thurgood

Special photography by Debbie Patterson

Quadrille

For Jean and Denis
for their unfailing help and support throughout this book

p. 1: *Crackle glaze and a hand-stamped blind on wardrobe shelving (pp. 60–3)*
pp. 2–3: *High-gloss lacquer on a set of drawers (pp. 56–7)*
p. 4: *Stencilled fruit on loom chairs (pp. 106–9)*
p. 5: *Gilded chequering on a circular table (pp. 75–7)*

Art Director: Mary Evans   **Studio Photography:** Nicki Dowey
Project Editor: Mary Davies   **Picture Researcher:** Helen Fickling
Art Editor: Rachel Gibson   **Production Manager:** Candida Lane

This edition first published in 2005 by Quadrille Publishing Limited
5th Floor, Alhambra House, 27–31 Charing Cross Road, London WC2H 0LS

British Library Cataloguing-in-Publication Data
A catalogue record for this book is available from the British Library.

ISBN-13: 978 184400 277 1
ISBN-10: 1 84400 277 2

Printed and bound in Spain

CONTENTS

INTRODUCTION

The purpose of this book is to explore ways of turning cast-off and budget-range furniture into functional pieces uniquely styled to suit your living spaces. Our aim is to provide you with a bank of inspirational ideas and technical advice on how to achieve custom-built results easily and cheaply.

How often have you scoured furniture shops and not found quite what you were looking for? Maybe the size or shape was wrong. Maybe the style or colour didn't complement your decor. Or maybe that wonderful character piece you discovered bore a ridiculous price tag.

As designers, we have strong views on what we want the furniture around us to look like and what we want it to do. Often making over other pieces, new or old, is the only affordable way to achieve both. For more years than I care to admit we had in one of our rooms at home a bulky, Gothic-style bed snapped up very cheaply in a weak moment at a furniture sale. When the old dinosaur finally became too much to bear, we chopped away the bulk of the head- and foot-boards, gilded it silver, using aluminium leaf, and dressed it in pale, floaty cotton for a soft, antique French look – a magical transformation and it cost us very little. So don't regard making over as a last resort. In the current shift towards simplicity in natural, uncluttered or minimal interiors for busy people living on tight budgets there is plenty of scope for painted and adapted furniture which exactly meets your needs with a personalized look that shop-bought furniture simply cannot have. The secret is to dream the dream and then have the confidence to make it real.

We find inspiration everywhere – in art and pattern books, in magazines, new and old, in visits to great houses and museums, even in jaunts to the cinema. I'm one of those irritating people likely to come out humming the set. There is a long history to draw upon since men and women began demanding more of their furniture than

Left: Heavily aged paint in a country setting: too extreme for all but the most romantic taste, it is a perfect demonstration of how and where paint breaks down on a much-used piece. To simulate the tones, I would try a base coat of ochre under top coats of aqua, grey and sombre green, separated by three wax-resist treatments (see page 144), and a lot of hard rubbing back.

Below: This pretty pie safe is more softly aged. A darker glaze (see page 147) could dull down the appealing two-colour scheme, and the swept top might be cut from MDF with strips of beading above and below the door.

Bright daubed paint and a pair of chunky cord handles lift a sturdy cupboard above the ordinary. This surprisingly harmonious effect is achieved by loosely following the order of the colours of the spectrum. To repeat, use artists' acrylic colours. For a less expensive alternative, you could try just two sections of the spectrum.

pure function, if, indeed, there was ever any distinction between function and form. I reckon that the world's first chair made some statement about the person who chose to live with it.

Your adaptations and paint and decorative finishes can be 'authentic' or high fantastical, grand or simple, even primitive. Until relatively recently in many parts of the world – in Poland, in Mexico and in the Indian sub-continent, for example – there have been vigorous and inspiring folk traditions of hand-painted furniture.

In our experience there are two important maxims to bear in mind in the search for suitable pieces to makeover. One, almost any surface can be prepared for painting so don't despair when confronted with plastic laminate. With a little imagination that seventies kitchen cabinet could turn country sophisticate or space-age futuristic. And two, style, even shape, isn't immutable. A little adaptation can create any number of new looks to fit granny's china cupboard for life in the fast lane.

INTRODUCTION

The very first step is to look at what you already have – the fittings you took on when you moved in, the cupboard you bought but never cared for, the table that no longer suits your taste or fills a space. Then, when friends or family offer you their rejects, look twice before you say no or hide them in the attic. Moving home can be a wonderful opportunity if you keep your mind open. What does it matter if someone's dump fest brings you a fifties chair crying out for retro decoupage?

Just one word of warning before you widen the hunt: no matter how much some carved oak wardrobe that's been in the family for decades seems to yearn for paint, think first. Genuine antiques and good furniture demand respect. We are not in the business of restoration so our house rule is simple. If the piece is sound and the style and wood are good, leave it for someone who will love it for itself. And if that turns out to be you, get expert advice for restoration.

The next place to look are the secondhand or junk shops. Get to know those in your local area. Do they specialize in certain kinds of stock?

Left: This almost monumental, custom-built piece suggests all kinds of ways in which a basic shape can be built up layer by layer using standard panels and mouldings from DIY stores. You could decorate with silver paint or metal leaf and finish with an ageing glaze (see pages 35 and 168).

Right: There's a confident colour sense and an eye for the potential in scrap material at work in these two makeovers with an ethnic feel. The wooden screen has been decoupaged (see page 160) with masses of intricate Indian cards, wrap and advertising. The simple chair is bound with strips of fabric, glued into place. I love the occasional buttons sewn on arms and legs.

Transformation time for some boring but sound laminate kitchen units (see page 89): masking, spray paints and varnish have created a tough surface, and new knobs and handles add the finishing touch.

Which day of the week does the new stock arrive? You need to be first on the doorstep to claim the pick of the crop. Chat to the proprietors and give them an idea of the kind of things you might be interested in. As you do your research, study prices. Whose are higher than average? Whose are low? Resist the temptation to snap up the first piece that matches your brief – it's galling to find a similar item down the road at half the price. But remember: market forces operate in this world too. If the look you want is trendy, you'll be hard pressed to find a bargain.

Local papers are another good hunting ground. Here you will find the dates of local auctions and, even better, a small ads section for unwanted items. If you are able to put in the time and can find suitable transport, this is the place to get a great bargain, simply by cutting out the middle man. Boot and garage sales offer the same incentive.

The other place to look is in the large retail outlets that produce budget ranges of new softwood and wood-based furniture. Their often basic shapes are an excellent starting point for adaptation and decoration, and as some are sold unfinished, protected with just a thin coat of PVA sealant, preparation is cut to the minimum – always a plus.

Making over old and new furniture is a great way to put a personal stamp on your surroundings. It can be a solitary pleasure or a companionable way to spend time with a partner or friend. With this book to inspire and encourage you, you have access to an almost unlimited range of possibilities. Enjoy.

PART ONE

PREPARATION

A guide to the tools, equipment and materials used to adapt and decorate furniture, plus detailed advice on preparing the surface and some of the techniques of simple adaptation

This kitchen-of-the-future suggests two interesting makeovers. First: the wavy table edge. Skim ply cut to shape with a jig saw and glued into place would be a good base for the mosaic. Note the repeat shape on the back of the unit, where a stouter, non-flexible material could be used. (Mosaic tiles seem to have been teamed with the opaque, coloured glass lozenges found in florists and specialist candle shops.) Second: the stainless steel sheeting on the doors. For safety's sake, ignore the cooker on casters and the part-tiled floor.

CLEANING
AND PREPARATION

You know it's true. Thorough cleaning and surface preparation are an essential part of any successful paint or decorative transformation so we make no apology for devoting the first six pages to what may seem an unexciting subject. The chart on pages 16–17 guides you through the treatment of most of the materials you are like to encounter as you reclaim and adapt old and budget-range furniture.

At the risk of putting you off before you've begun, do be aware that junk furniture will more often than not be dirty, even greasy, when you find it. It makes sense to do the first cleaning stage outdoors if you can, and those of a nervous disposition should bribe someone else to make a first foray with a stiff wire brush.

Most of the materials and equipment you need are very familiar, even household objects – some you may have already. Others, such as protective masks and goggles, are perhaps less obvious but important. Don't allow some long-experienced do-it-yourselfer to persuade you otherwise. Buy approved-standard masks and goggles if you can. They are not expensive and you will use them again and again.

PROTECTION
Preparing surfaces can be messy, even hazardous work so don't forget to protect youself and your home. Cotton aprons or overalls and rubber gloves are great for most undertakings. Masks help cut down the risk of inhaling dust as you rub down (see also page 18) and protect against harmful vapours, but you need stout plastic goggles too. Cotton and plastic dustsheets come in various sizes. But beware: liquids can 'pool' on plastic.

CLEANING AND RUBBING DOWN

Dusters, a plastic washing-up bowl, household sponge and scourer should all be part of your basic kit. Never throw cotton shirts or sheets away. Tear and store – they make wonderful lint-free rags. Sugar soap solution is best for degreasing surfaces, though you can substitute detergent. Several rinses with clean water are essential.

Wirewool cleans and provides a key for paint on metal and plastics; use with white spirit (top right). Buy loose in small bales or try the synthetic pad form. Sandpaper needs little introduction. Fine and medium grades are the two you are likely to need, but both clog quickly, must be used dry and create dust so don't choose them if you suspect the paint is lead based. Modern gloss paint is leadfree, but be wary of old painted furniture. The grey wet and dry papers illustrated here are used wet and do not cause dust.

Chemical paint strippers are the best way to remove paint or varnish, and methylated spirits will clean metals such as zinc or tin.

SIMPLE REPAIRS

Don't take on any piece which is structurally unsound – it is not worth spending time and money on something which may not in the end be able to perform as well as you hoped. Minor surface damage can be repaired (see pages 16–17 for specific advice) or may even enhance some of the ageing techniques in Part Three, and, as the project illustrated on page 67 makes clear, a wrecked door need not defeat you. Once wood-based surfaces are thoroughly clean and before repairing, check carefully for woodworm. If you find any suspect holes – they are round and approx. 2mm (¹⁄₁₆in) in diameter – brush all surfaces twice with a woodworm killer and inject into all holes.

FILLING HOLES AND CRACKS

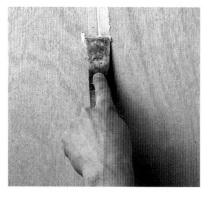

Wood and wood-based material
Apply flexible, ready-mixed filler with a filler knife, spreading downwards from the top. Overfill, removing any obvious excess quickly and smoothing to make sanding easier.

Laminate
Using car-body filler and a spatula, fill damaged sections by spreading downwards and then smoothing with a horizontal stroke. This dual action consolidates and flattens for sanding.

SECURING RAISED LAMINATE

1 Apply wood glue liberally to the base to which the laminate is to be attached, making sure the surface is completely covered.
Note To secure a new sheet of laminate to a surface, use contact adhesive (see page 27).

2 Position appropriate pieces of batten and one or more G-clamps to ensure that the whole section is kept completely flat while it dries. Use a rag to wipe off excess glue before drying begins, taking care not to disturb the clamp.

MENDING A WOBBLY CHAIR LEG

Find the point of weakness – it is sure to be a corner joint – and drill four pilot holes, two in each visible, outer side of the upright. They must be positioned in alternate planes so that the countersunk screws will pass through the upright into the adjacent side of the seat base. Insert and tighten the screws to secure. Smooth wood filler over the screw heads to conceal. **Note** For clarity, only two screws are shown.

REMOVING OLD NAILS

Nail with no head

If pliers are no use, place a thin piece of wood beside the nail to protect the surface and create purchase. Bend with a claw hammer as shown and then pull and twist until released.

Nail with a head

Grasp the head of the nail with a claw hammer, again protecting the surface with a thin piece of wood, and lever it out by firmly rocking the tool forwards from claw to hammer head.

REPLACING DAMAGED HINGES

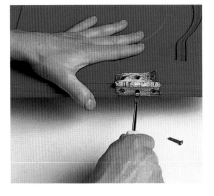

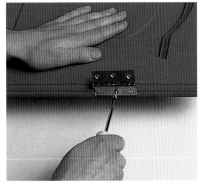

1 Take care not to damage the wood as you unscrew. Throw away screws as well as hinges.
2 Screw in the new hinges, using the old holes. Screw heads must lie flush or the door will bind.

To correct, buy screws one gauge smaller. If the screws do not fit firmly, pad the holes with tiny dowels. For a stronger hinge, choose a longer one, but beware – it will be wider too.

PREPARING THE SURFACE

All the standard surfaces are listed below. Seek expert advice from a local DIY store if you cannot find the one you want. Dip stripping is not an option for large pieces of furniture – it may cause warping or loose joints. Untreated live knots in new wood will create dark patches in paint over time so apply knotting fluid before you paint. Treating knots which are oozing resin is a long process. Avoid that section if you can.

SURFACE	CLEAN/ DEGREASE	REPAIR/ FILL	RUB DOWN/SAND after repair and/or construction	PRIMER/ UNDERCOAT
WOOD Painted emulsion or gloss **Sealed** with PVA adhesive **Waxed**	Wash with sugar-soap solution, using lint-free rag, and leave to dry.	Fill holes with fine-grade flexible wood filler.	**Sound surfaces** Emulsion/sealed/ waxed: Use fine-grade sandpaper to provide key for painting. Gloss paint: Use wet and dry paper for key. **Unsound surfaces** Take off flaky or rough paint with a scraper; for obstinate areas use a chemical gel or paste paint stripper.	**Waxed surfaces** Rub a thin film of dry domestic or toilet soap all over the surface and then treat as appropriate (see below). **Sound surfaces** Unnecessary **Bare patches** Spot 'prime' with appropriate material: • acrylic wood primer (w) Allow to dry (2 hours). • oil-based u/coat (o) Allow to dry (16 hours).
Varnished	Brush well with stiff-bristled brush and then wash as above.	See above.	**Sound surfaces** See emulsion/sealed/ waxed above. **Unsound surfaces** See Unsound surfaces above. Alternative: varnish remover.	See Sound surfaces and Bare patches above.
Unpainted	Wipe with damp, lint-free rag. Do not soak – water will raise grain and may cause wood to warp.	See above. Alternative: all-purpose filler. **New wood** Apply knotting to prevent sap seepage.	Use fine-grade sandpaper to provide key for painting.	'Prime' with appropriate material: • acrylic wood primer (w) • oil-based u/coat (o) See above for drying times.
MDF Painted	See Wood, painted.	Fill holes with fine-grade flexible wood filler or all-purpose filler.	See above.	**Sound surfaces** Unnecessary **Bare patches** See below.
Unpainted	See Wood, unpainted.	See above.	Use fine-grade sandpaper to provide key for painting. Be gentle: MDF cannot be made smoother by sanding.	'Prime' with appropriate material: • acrylic wood primer (w) • emulsion (w) • oil-based u/coat (o) Emulsion drying time: 2–3 hours.
PLYWOOD Painted	See Wood, painted.	See above.	Use fine-grade sandpaper to provide key for painting.	See MDF, painted.

• Clean again after rubbing down/sanding. Use warm, soapy water and lint-free rag.
• Use a mask if sanding, rubber gloves if working with white spirit or paint strippers. Good ventilation is vital at all times.

SURFACE	CLEAN/ DEGREASE	REPAIR/ FILL	RUB DOWN/SAND after repair and/or construction	PRIMER/ UNDERCOAT
PLYWOOD Varnished	See Wood, varnished.	See MDF, painted.	See Plywood, painted.	See Wood, painted (Sound surfaces and Bare patches).
Unpainted	See Wood, unpainted.	See above.	See above.	See Wood, unpainted.
CHIPBOARD Wood veneered (inc. ash, pine, mahogany, teak)	See Wood, as appropriate.	See above.	See above.	See Wood, as appropriate.
Melamine-coated (white, black, wood effect)	Wash with sugar-soap solution, using lint-free rag, and leave to dry.	See above.	See above.	See Wood, unpainted.
HARDBOARD Painted	See MDF, painted.	See MDF, painted.	See MDF, painted.	See MDF, painted.
LAMINATES AND PLASTICS (inc. wood effects on chipboard, hardboard and plywood)	Wash with sugar-soap solution or wipe clean with white spirit, using wirewool, and leave to dry.	Fill cracks and holes with car-body filler.	Use wet and dry paper to provide key for painting.	See Wood, unpainted.
FERROUS METAL (e.g. iron and steel) **Bare**	Wipe with white spirit, using wirewool, and leave to dry. **Heavy rust** Rub down with wire brush before cleaning as above.	See above.	See above.	Prime with either: • metal primer ⓞ Allow to dry (12 hours). • red oxide primer ⓞ Allow to dry (16 hours). Follow with universal acrylic primer if using water-based paint.
Lacquered, painted or plastic-coated	**Sound** Wash with sugar-soap solution and leave to dry. **Unsound** Use a chemical stripper to remove the covering.	See above.	See above.	**Sound surfaces** Unnecessary **Bare patches** Spot 'prime' as above.
NON-FERROUS METAL (e.g. aluminium, chrome plating, tin and zinc)	Wipe with white spirit or methylated spirits, using wirewool, wash with detergent and leave to dry.	See above.	See above.	Prime with: • metal primer ⓞ Allow to dry (12 hours). Follow with universal acrylic primer if using water-based paint.
RATTAN, RUSH, WILLOW AND OTHER BASKET WEAVE	Wash with sugar-soap solution, using lint-free rag, and leave to dry fully. Do not soak.	Seek expert advice.	**Rush (sealed or painted)** Use very fine wirewool very gently to provide key for painting. **Rattan and Willow (sealed or painted)** See Rush. Or use very fine sandpaper very gently. **Unsealed and unpainted** Unnecessary	**New surfaces** Unnecessary **Painted surfaces** Prime with either: • acrylic spray primer ⓦ • acrylic wood primer ⓦ Apply with brush to heavily painted surfaces.

- Clean again after rubbing down/sanding. Use warm, soapy water and lint-free rag.
- Use a mask if sanding, rubber gloves if working with white spirit or paint strippers. Good ventilation is vital at all times.

ⓦ = water-based ⓞ = oil-based   Water-based primers/undercoats for water-based finishes; oil-based primers/undercoats for oil-based finishes

MATERIALS

Good woodyards and DIY stores will hold all the stock you need and can give valuable advice. We have incorporated some of the commonest materials into our adaptations, but it is well worth looking around to see what else is available. Stores are now much more aware of changing tastes and trends, and browsing will spark all sorts of ideas.

The wood and wood-based boards we list are available in various thicknesses. The sizes we suggest were chosen to suit both the function and look we wanted for a specific piece of furniture. You must judge what will suit yours. We favour MDF, or medium-density fibreboard, above plywood for most adaptations on painted furniture. It can be shaped so easily with a jig saw without splintering and its ultra-smooth surface is a delight to paint or stain. Composed of wood fibres bonded with synthetic resins, wax and formaldehyde, it produces a fine dust when worked so, as with all solid timber and wood-based materials, you must take precautions when cutting or drilling (see the chart opposite). Fortunately sanding only makes it rougher, not smoother, which cuts preparation time.

MDF (left) AND PLYWOOD
MDF's smooth face and profile create the better surface for paint. Three ply is the most familiar form of plywood. Ultra-thin skim ply is used for curved surfaces. Unlike MDF, ply can simply be varnished.

WORKING WITH TIMBER AND WOOD-BASED MATERIALS

Wear protective clothing
- Goggles
- Disposable face mask manufactured to approved standard
- Gloves and long sleeves for those with sensitive skin

Work outside or in a well-ventilated area
- Cover carpets and furniture with dustsheets
- Avoid sources of heat or ignition

Dispose of waste in sealed plastic bags
- Damp dust with fine spray
- Sweep carefully
- Vacuum

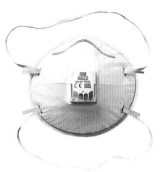

A mask manufactured to approved standard

BATTENS
Made of softwood, standard batten is square or rectangular and is available in a range of sizes. It has many uses, including edging on wood-based material and support for shelves or when fitting extra pieces of wood. Quadrant batten, of soft or hardwood, is used to cover joins and retain glass.

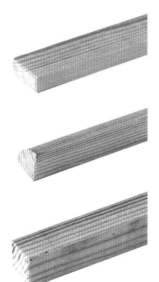

DOWELS
Useful for curtain poles and (see page 130) bed posts, hardwood dowels are widely available in various diameters from 6mm to 25mm (¼–1in). Softwood versions can be found in some larger sizes. Short sections of the smallest sizes are used to plug worn screw holes (see page 15).

KNOW YOUR WOOD

SOFTWOOD	HARDWOOD
From coniferous trees	**From broad-leaved trees**
Pine	Beech
Fir	Mahogany
Spruce	Oak
	Ramin
	Teak
Description	**Description**
• More easily dented – paint and varnish increase resistance	• Stronger – more resistant to damage and carries heavier loads without bending
• Unpainted wood darkens quickly in direct sunlight	
• Widely available in many sizes	• Apart from mouldings, available only from specialist suppliers
Handling characteristics	**Handling characteristics**
• Easy to smooth by sanding	• Easy to glue
• Live knots must be treated before painting (see page 16)	• Harder to screw into – use drill for pilot holes
• Easy to glue, screw into or nail – use bradawl for pilot holes	• Avoid nailing (danger of splits) – drill pilot holes if essential
• Easy to stain or varnish	• Responds well to stain or polish

EDGE TRIMS
Decorative fretwork is available in a wide variety of styles and is usually sold by the metre. Woodyards will stock a range but for a wider selection approach the specialist mail-order companies. Mostly made from MDF, fretwork is easy to cut to length with a tenon saw and can be used to trim shelves, doors and simple cupboards. You can finish it with emulsion, oil or any other paint.

MOULDINGS
Obtainable in a variety of styles and designs, some mouldings can be used as another form of edge trim or for adding panels to flush doors. Others can be combined to reshape a piece completely (see page 8). Sold by the metre, they are available in hard and softwood from woodyards, DIY stores and framing suppliers. The hardwood versions will be more expensive so, if you have a choice, don't buy them when you plan to paint.

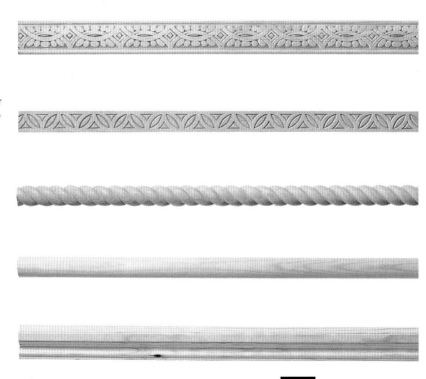

METAL: SHEET, MESH AND WIRE Chicken wire makes a cheap mesh for use indoors when sprayed with metallic paint. Good DIY stores will carry a variety of decorative meshes and wires for the same purpose. Chicken wire is usually sold in rolls, meshes by the sheet. The zinc and tin plate used to cover surfaces and for punched-tin effects are also often sold by the sheet. You can reduce the sheen of either (see the darker sample) by rubbing with wirewool, used alone or with a little white spirit.

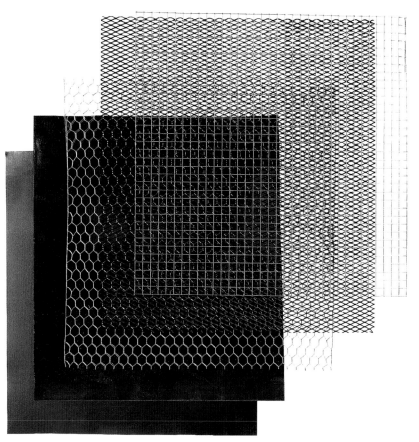

APPLYING CHROME TRIM

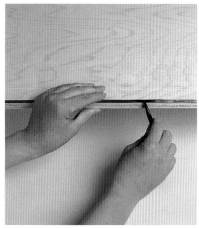

1 Peeling off a little of the backing at a time, press the self-adhesive strip firmly onto the smooth edge. Continue in this way, holding the trim in one hand and pressing with the other, until the piece has been positioned or until you need to cut to fit.

2 Cut (if required) with scissors and press into place. Use the rounded handle of a knife or fork (sometimes, as here, a tool is provided) to smooth gently along its length, removing any bumps. Several narrow strips were laid here for a ridged effect. Wider strips are also available.

CUTTING WOOD

Experienced do-it-yourselfers may find little that is new in this and some of the following sections, which are designed very largely to encourage those less familiar with the equipment and techniques associated with adapting old and budget furniture. But don't skip them entirely – there may be something here for you.

All but the most practically challenged probably own a saw. If you don't, a hand saw is not a major expense. Jig saws are more expensive but they certainly make long cuts on MDF and plywood much easier and, once you are confident, they are a dream if you want to create decorative shapes quickly and easily. They can be hired at a daily rate from tool-hire shops and, when you are not sure how you will make out, it is sensible to test drive one for a day. If you don't have the luxury of a permanent work table, you might like to invest in an adjustable work bench. Available at all good DIY stores, even the most basic provides a stable surface to which you can clamp materials for cutting or drilling. However, it is best to lay large sheets on the floor, supported on battens arranged in the direction of the cut but out of reach. Make sure there is nothing underneath that might be damaged.

WORKING WITH HAND AND POWER SAWS

See the safety chart on page 19, and that for working with power tools on page 29. Never work in a cramped area, and make sure the light is good. Tuck all wires and cables out of the way. Check that tools are in working order and, if using clamps, that they are firmly tightened. Before cutting, use a straight-edged piece of paper to confirm that the ends of dowels and battens are true. Coated or veneered chipboard chips on the underside edge when sawed by hand so draw cut lines on the side that will be visible. Reverse, drawing cut lines on the invisible side, when using a jig saw.

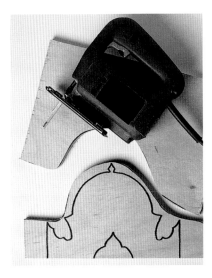

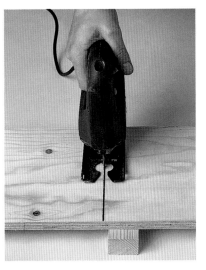

Cutting out detailed shapes

Begin by cutting away the excess material in a series of simple cuts. Then cut out the detail. This also applies to working with a coping saw – the hand tool used for shaping wood.

Cutting out accurately

Use a soft pencil to mark the cutting line clearly and cut on the waste side of it. If you cut on the pencil line, the piece will be a little shorter than you intended.

Using a tenon saw

The short, straight, rectangular blade makes this an easier saw to control than the longer, more flexible panel saw, and it also cuts through plywood and thin board more easily. It is for these reasons that we recommend it to the beginner who needs to buy a hand saw. To begin a cut, grip the saw firmly, extending your first finger along the side of the handle, place the saw at the forward edge of the marked line (see left and above) and draw it back towards you a couple of times to ease the teeth into a better position before you begin to saw.

USING METAL

Inexpensive metal detail has been used for many centuries to add character and charm to simple furniture and smaller decorative objects so there's much to learn from the folk cultures of Asia, Europe and the Americas. But it's probably retro chic and specifically the utility look of the fifties diner which has prompted the current craze for metal-covered worktops. The tools you need for our metal-based techniques – fitting wire inserts, punching tin and covering surfaces – are all widely available, inexpensive and easy to use. For information on materials, see pages 21 and 40 and the adhesives chart on page 27.

METALWORKING Masking and gaffer tape to cover sharp edges and position designs; a hand-held staple gun to secure chicken wire (and fabric); cotton gloves to prevent grease build-up; a tile cutter (centre) to score surfaces; a nail punch (below) plus hammer to punch tin; a bolster chisel to define creases in zinc (see opposite); heavy-duty tin snips to cut sheet metal; a junior hacksaw to cut metal rod; a rubber mallet to flatten cut edges

SHAPING AND BENDING A ZINC SHEET

1 Zinc needs a little persuasion to bend cleanly and accurately. For more about the technique of covering a work surface, see the French Dresser project on pages 73–4 (Preparing the zinc and Fixing the zinc). Once any necessary cuts have been made to aid folding and all the edges have been tapped with a rubber mallet to flatten, position a metal ruler along each fold line in turn while you score the metal lightly with a tile cutter. Practise the technique on a piece of scrap first – too much pressure and you may cut too far through the metal.

2 Grasping the bolster chisel by its shaft, place its tip on one of the scored lines and tap the other end with the hammer. Reposition the chisel, repeating to improve the crease along the whole line. Repeat on all fold lines.

3 Position the zinc on the surface, right side up. Using a batten approx. 30.5cm (12in) long as a cushion between hammer and metal, tap along the edges of the surface to bend the zinc down as you create the first fold on each side.

WORKING WITH METAL

- Always wear goggles.
- Cover raw edges of tin or zinc with masking tape to avoid cuts.
- Never fully close tin snips when cutting metal.
- Wear heavy-duty gardening gloves when cutting chicken wire.
- Use pliers to bend cut ends of chicken wire inwards to prevent grazes.
- Place a tab of masking tape at drilling point to prevent bit from slipping.
- Make pilot hole with centre punch and hammer before drilling through or into metal.
- Sand or file exposed cut edges on finished work to smooth.

JOINING 1

Screws are conventionally measured by length and by the diameter or gauge of the upper, unthreaded section (or shank). The longer or wider a screw is, the greater its fixing strength. Most of the screws we use in our projects are gauge 6 or 8. The screw most commonly used today, which we recommend for all practical purposes, is the countersunk wood or chipboard screw with no shank, available with philips or pozidrive cross head. Countersunk heads are designed to lie flush so you need a hand tool or drill bit to bore space for the head. The cross-head type will be determined by the screwdriver you use. Single-slot heads are now used largely for decoration or to match existing screws. Panel pins are the only practical nails we use here; the copper roof nails must be trimmed with a single oblique cut to fit.

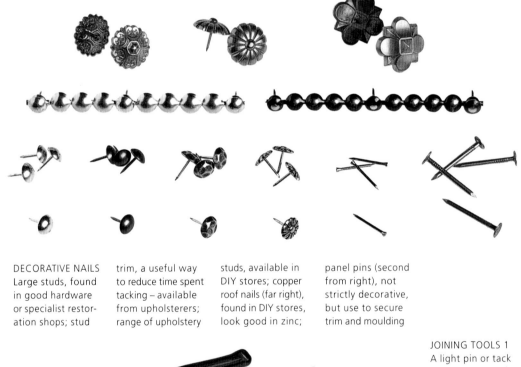

DECORATIVE NAILS Large studs, found in good hardware or specialist restoration shops; stud trim, a useful way to reduce time spent tacking – available from upholsterers; range of upholstery studs, available in DIY stores; copper roof nails (far right), found in DIY stores, look good in zinc; panel pins (second from right), not strictly decorative, but use to secure trim and moulding

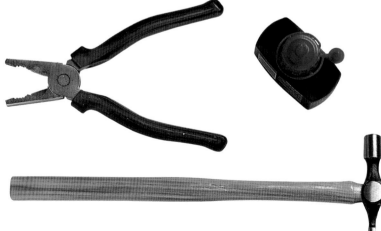

JOINING TOOLS 1 A light pin or tack hammer is ideal for our adaptations. The narrow section opposite the head, called the cross pein, is used for starting off panel pins held between the fingers. Invest in a good pair of pliers – you can use them to trim the shafts of nails that are too long. Brush wood glue onto battens and mouldings before panel pinning.

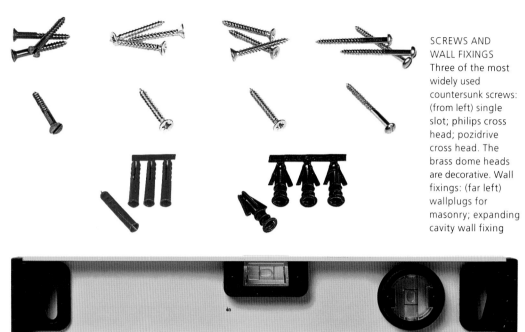

SCREWS AND WALL FIXINGS Three of the most widely used countersunk screws: (from left) single slot; philips cross head; pozidrive cross head. The brass dome heads are decorative. Wall fixings: (far left) wallplugs for masonry; expanding cavity wall fixing

Single-slot head	Pozidrive head	Philips head

JOINING TOOLS 2 A spirit level for checking alignment; a screwdriver – you can buy both single and rachet types for interchangeable heads; a counter-sinking tool to prepare headroom for countersunk screws; a bradawl to make small holes in softwood and metal

WHICH ADHESIVE?

JOIN	TO			
	WOOD-BASED MATERIALS inc. laminates	PLASTICS inc. laminates	METALS	ADHESIVE TYPE
Ceramic	✓	✓	✓	**Ceramic tile adhesive** Thick paste dries white. Also use for beads & shells. **PVA high-bond adhesive & sealer** Dries clear.
Fabric	✓	✓	✓	**Fabric glue** See also PVA adhesive.
Metal	✓	✓	✓	**Contact adhesive** Applied to both surfaces. Dries clear.
Paper	✓	✓	✓	**PVA adhesive or white glue** Dries clear. Dilute with water to stiffen fabric for decorative detail (see page 116). See also Spray mount.
Plant material	✓	✓	✗	Flat material: **Spray mount** Bulkier material: **Photo mount** Temporary bonding for masking with leaves or cut paper.
Plastic	✓	✓	✗	New laminate: As Metal. Repair: As Wood, light duty (no pins).
Wood	✓	✓	✗	Light duty: **PVA wood glue plus panel pins** Dries clear Heavy duty: **Quick-dry epoxy glue** Two-part mix dries clear.

JOINING 2

The tiny head of a panel pin is almost invisible when hammered firmly into position. If you want to conceal it completely, you can use a small nail punch to drive it below the surface and fill the hole with flexible wood filler but that's probably unnecessary for all practical purposes if you plan to paint. Nail the thinner material to the thicker and, for strength, where possible choose a nail at least twice as long as the thickness of the piece to be secured. When nailing thin pieces or near the end of timber, blunt the tip of the pin or nail with a hammer to avoid splits and bore a small pilot hole with a bradawl.

When using screws, again choose one at least twice as long as the piece to be secured. To screw one piece of wood to another, you need two pilot holes for ease of entry. They should be narrower and (in total) shorter than the screw so that the thread has something to bite on. First mark the screw position with a pencil cross on the piece to be secured and drill a hole through it, using an appropriate bit. This is the time to use a countersink bit or tool if required, checking the depth with the screw. Position the two pieces with the drilled section on top and mark the lower pilot hole by pushing a bradawl or pencil through the hole. Remove the upper piece and drill the second hole. Realign the two pieces, insert the screw and use a hand or powered driver to secure.

Brass screws are softer than steel ones so prepare the thread by screwing in and removing a steel screw of the same size first to reduce the risk of damaging or breaking the head. Take advice when fixing to walls. Tapping will determine whether it's a solid or cavity surface, but you must choose between a range of cavity fittings that spread the load.

POWER DRILL
Powered drills and drill/drivers can speed many joining jobs. Shown here is a standard drill and selection of drill bits for working in wood and metal. Also shown is the chuck key, which on this model is required to change the bits. Some have a built-in fitting that allows for easier changing of bits. A variety of drills and drill/drivers is available. Check the bits included; separate sets are also available.

WORKING WITH HAND AND POWER DRILLS

Make sure work is securely clamped to a stable surface. Insert a piece of wood between the clamp and work to prevent damage to the surface. You could hire or buy a drill stand to ensure that the holes you drill are straight but there are cheaper solutions. Keep the drill at chest height. Hold it parallel to your body when drilling downwards, as onto a work bench. Hold it at a right angle to your body when drilling a hole in front of you, as into a wall. Standing a try square on end by the drill also helps. To drill to an exact depth, place tape on the drill bit at the required length so you know when to stop (see below). To prevent slippage when drilling laminate, start the hole with a bradawl or nail.

Drilling a large hole in a dowel
Screw a length of 25 x 50mm (1 x 2in) batten wide side down to a wider length of scrap wood as above. Position the dowel below the batten and secure, using a large G-clamp. This simple device will hold a dowel firmly without slippage while you work. The illustration to the right shows a flat wood (or spade) bit in use.

USING POWER TOOLS

- Use circuit breaker to cut off current in case saw or drill cuts cable.
- Ban children and pets from working area.
- Check blade is facing in right direction.
- Replace blunt blades and drill bits.
- Check there is nothing underneath which could be cut by blade or bit.
- Wear goggles.
- Keep cable away from blade or bit.
- Switch off before removing from wood.
- Unplug when tool is not in use or when changing blades and bits.

PLANNING

Most of the planning tools and materials we use are very basic. In many instances the traditional carpenters' and graphite pencils shown below could be replaced with a thick, soft lead pencil. Layout and tracing paper are available in various sizes – A4, A3 and A2 are all useful and can be found in artists' supplies shops. So can the wonderful matt transfer film (see opposite). Graph paper is a help when checking design proportions or planning adapations of your own. Use a scale of 1:10 if working with metric measurements; 1:12 is more convenient if working with the imperial system. For space reasons we don't show our larger straight edge – a 2m (6ft 6in) long piece of 50 x 25mm (2 x 1in) pine kept strictly for drawing long, straight lines. There are various ways to check the right angles on guide lines for painted panels, mouldings and grid patterns – including T-squares and try squares – but we reckon a set square is one of the cheapest solutions and all you need for our projects. A spirit level is vital too, if marking the position, for example, of wall fittings; there's one illustrated on page 27.

PLANNING TOOLS A metal ruler, a good straight edge but beware – it can be bent or twisted; an extending metal ruler; graph, tracing and layout papers; coloured pencils, useful for hiding the grid lines for roller patterns; marker pen; carpenters' and (far right) graphite pencils, both for marking wood; Chinagraph pencil for marking dark surfaces, glass and fabric; a set square. Not shown: permanent pen, another way to mark metal

USING MASKS FOR SIMPLE AND COMPLEX SHAPES

MATERIALS
Newspaper, the cheapest way to protect the area around a stencil card when using sprays; low-tack brown paper masking, a good way to create straight-sided shapes; masking tape, available in various widths, but remove some of the tack if using on paint; matt transfer film, the most expensive and most flexible mask (see below)

Using a brown paper mask

1 Two horizontal strips were cut and stuck down, placing the taped sections (see right) to the edges of the rectangle. Two verticals were positioned in the same way.

2 To remove, hold the paper sections and pull gently so the tape does not disturb the sprayed paint. When working with multiple strips, make sure they are removed in reverse order. This secure system is cheaper than masking tape.

Using matt transfer film

This matt, low-tack film with a translucent paper backing enables you to create curved or intricate masks by tracing directly onto the film. It is available in a variety of sizes. Simply place it over your chosen design, trace the outline, cut out with a scalpel, carefully peel off the backing and position. The pineapple was composed of several pieces but I retained the background too so I had two options – to mask all but the fruit or just the fruit. You can also draw shapes straight onto the film.

MIXING COLOUR

Most of the paint, glaze and wash colours featured on our painted projects are mixed from a base of modern, water-based vinyl emulsion, tinted with water-based artists' acrylic colours (available in tubes in a wide range of tones under standard names). I like to work with vinyl emulsion because it is easy and safe to use, quick to dry and almost odourfree.

Although I choose to mix most of my colours when working with emulsion, there are occasions when I opt for premixed tones. The exceptions are the deep reds, oranges, yellows and blues, and the coats used before and after crackle varnish. Deep tones require so much colour if mixed from a white base that the paint's plasticity is compromised, that is, it no longer flows properly. Similarly, water-based crackle varnish can't work its intended magic (see page 148) when the paint above and below it is behaving unpredictably. The alternative when you plan to use strong tones could be to go for a base nearer to the colour you want. But strong colours are the most fugitive so I often prefer to avoid the risk of upsetting the composition of the paint.

It's easy to modify the colours I suggest and to experiment with your own. Add each ingredient in stages, stir well and check the effect as you go. Black and white will darken or lighten some tones but shades of grey create subtler results, and you can add a little water (or thinner) to help the paint flow more easily. Keep records of what you do and mix slightly more than you think you need. Manufacturers estimate that emulsion covers 9–15m^2 (11–18yd^2). Actual coverage varies according to usage and surface. Added colour and scumble glaze make no real difference.

Most period colour ranges are modern vinyl emulsions. Seek advice from the manufacturer on suitable colouring agents if you want to use traditional-type water-based paints. If you want to use an eggshell base, the colouring agent must be oil-based too, and use white spirit to thin. Don't try colour mixing with gloss paints.

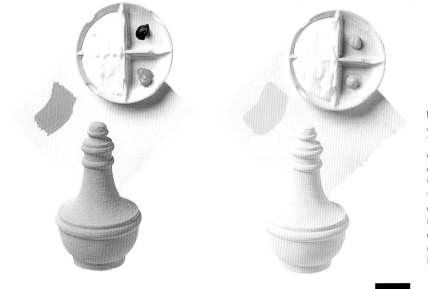

MIXING FROM A WHITE BASE Tones of artists' acrylic colour were added to white vinyl matt emulsion to create both colours: (left) monestial and emerald greens; cadmium and lemon yellows.

MIXING FROM A DARK BASE

Start from a dark base if you want a dark colour. Here the cadmium red of the centre finial has been modified (left) to a warm, mid-range brown with payne's grey, while (right) burnt umber has created a darker, earthier tone. Much smaller quantities of greys and umbers are also used to reduce colour intensity.

WASHES, WAXES AND GLAZES

A pale blue artists' colour was mixed with (left to right) water, furniture wax and transparent acrylic scumble glaze for three very different effects (and tones). Acrylic colour was used for finials 1 and 3, but working with wax meant a switch to oil. Note the grain visible through the wash on finial 1. Scumble glaze also makes paint appear translucent, an effect utilized in the colourwash finish on finial 3.

MEDIUM	COLOUR WITH	THIN WITH
WATER-BASED		
• Vinyl matt emulsion • Vinyl silk emulsion • Acrylic scumble glaze • Acrylic varnishing wax	• Artists' acrylic colour	• Water
OIL-BASED		
• Furniture wax	• Artists' oil colour	• White spirit

SPECIALIST PAINTS

Gilding doesn't have to mean 'gold'. You can achieve convincing silver, copper and bronze finishes with the leaf, paint, cream and bronze powders I use in our projects. Materials have improved enormously in the past few years. But, if you decide to use dutch metal leaf, be sure to buy the loose type. Transfer leaf, mounted on film, is difficult to handle. I'm rapidly becoming a spray-paint freak too. Applied lightly for good, even coverage and sealed with an appropriate varnish, spray paints are the best way I've found to cover difficult makeover surfaces like plastic laminate. If you have difficulty finding products locally, consult the stockists list on page 188 – many companies have mail-order services.

FABRIC COLOURS
Fabric paints come in liquid or pen forms. Liquid forms are available in a range of colours and effects (opaque, translucent or textured) and can be applied with a fine artists' or stencil brush. Pen forms are just like markers. Both must be sealed with an iron on the reverse. Dyes are made for cold-water hand or machine washing (see page 94).

WORKING WITH SPRAY PAINTS

Diffused colour

A soft-edged look can be achieved with two steady, sweeping strokes but don't press hard. Hold the can 30.5cm (12in) from the surface.

Solid colour

You need up to ten sweeping strokes for such opaque coverage. Again, don't be tempted to press hard. Aim for a series of light, even coats.

WORKING WITH GILDED FINISHES

MATERIALS
From the left: Loose gold dutch metal leaf, made from three cheaper metals and available in various tones, here interleaved for easier use; liquid leaf paint, expensive because it is powdered gold in a medium but economical to use; bronze powders for gold, copper and bronze effects (in paper packets and tube) – masks are essential when using them; gilt cream, a good alternative to leaf, easy to apply and available in various tones; silver and gold acrylic paint, much improved in quality, easy to use and quick drying

Applying dutch metal leaf

1 Using a fitch, brush an even coat of size onto the areas you intend to gild. Wait until the size becomes clear and tacky (15–20 minutes).

2 Lift each leaf carefully, making sure you pick up only one at a time, and place on the sized area. Smooth and then burnish, working gently with a soft-bristled brush or duster.

PAINTING EQUIPMENT

Most of the tools I use in our projects are inexpensive and can be bought from any DIY store if you don't already have them. Some of the pure bristle brushes are more costly and you'll find them in good hardware or artists' supplies shops. It's worth assembling a basic kit so that you can tackle most makeovers easily. Do use the equipment specified for a technique or you may not achieve the intended effect. Ordinary household sponges, for example, have their uses, but when a project asks for sea sponges it is worth spending that little bit more. You can, however, make savings on the number of brushes I specify by cleaning the brush used for a previous stage and doubling up.

With care, good brushes will last a long time. Clean them thoroughly. For water-based materials, rinse under running water, wash in soapy water and rinse again. Then rub the bristles between your palms inside a bin liner, reshape while damp and hang to dry. For oil-based materials, dip and rinse in methylated spirits, squeezing hard to clean before washing in soapy water, rinsing and reshaping as above. Some specialist paints require paint thinners for cleaning – I also recommend thinners to clean tin when finishing. Use with great care and follow the manufacturer's instructions for storage.

CLOTHS, SPONGES AND ROLLERS Mutton cloth, sold on the roll and very inexpensive – ideal for applying waxes; a lint-free cotton cloth, also used for applying waxes and for removing excess paint and glaze; sea sponges, whose irregular texture creates attractive effects when used to apply paint or glaze to wood or fabric; a synthetic sponge and two sponge refits for paint rollers, useful for improvised stamps; a wallpaper seam roller, the easiest way to create striped patterns

BRUSHES FOR SURFACES
From the top: two round hoghair brushes, good for stippling and for textural finishes; a varnish brush, expensive and best kept for acrylic varnishes; two emulsion brushes, whose especially flexible bristles are ideal for applying water-based paint; two household brushes, basic, stiff-bristled brushes for gloss paint, oil-based varnish and 'dirty jobs'; plus metal and plastic paint kettles – use the plastic, lidded type for storing water-based paints and glazes; mixing sticks, a good use for scrap wood

BRUSHES FOR DECORATION
From top left: Three stencil brushes, inexpensive so it's good to keep a range of sizes; selection of five small artists' brushes, plus (the longest) a round fitch – all are good for freehand painting and the fitch is also used to apply wax resist and glue; a lining brush, whose long, pure bristles are best when painting long, straight, thin lines; two soft-bristled brushes, used to apply dutch metal leaf and bronze powders

STAMPS, STENCILS AND DECOUPAGE

There are no surprises in the materials and equipment lists for these familiar techniques, and everything you need can be found in any crafts or artists' supplies shop.

Rubber stamps are now available in a huge range of designs and styles and offer an attractive, easy option if you want to decorate painted (or unpainted) surfaces. You can apply liquid stamp paints with a roller, but I much prefer the water-based ink stamp pads for fabric that work on wood, metal and plastics as well and make the best impressions. See page 164 for more about stamps, bought and improvised.

A scalpel (or craft knife) and cutting mat are essential when making stencils. You can cut them from paper, postcard-weight card or oiled-manilla stencil card. Stencil card, available in various sizes, is obviously the most expensive, but it is the strongest and certainly worth buying if you plan to use a design frequently. Of course, if you have linseed oil to hand, you could try sealing plain light card for yourself, but do make sure it is completely dry before you use it.

Decoupage depends for its impact largely on the materials you choose. Dover publish invaluable compilations of out-of-copyright material, and, as the screen on page 8 suggests, there's a wealth of contemporary ephemera just begging to be exploited.

STAMPS
Rubber stamps will produce hard-wearing results on any prepared and painted surface if you use a water-based fabric ink stamp pad and seal. Subtle colours are available, and the stamps are easily cleaned with soapy water. Use the plain end of a sponge roller for a perfect spot.

USING REGISTER MARKS FOR STENCILS

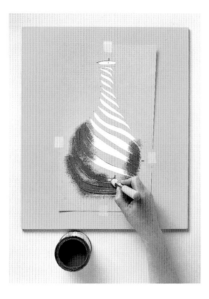

Note the aligning pencil marks at the top. The lower one indicates the centre top of the basic white vase shape and was transferred from the stencil to the shape once the paint had dried. Its position is important because you must be able to align the first mark with the one on the second stencil once that is in position. Registration marks have also been added at the sides and centre bottom. All will be concealed by the second stencil colour.

AGEING EFFECTS FOR DECOUPAGE

Discoloration

Prepare tea, using two bags to each half cup of water. Cool without stirring. Pour off the liquid and wipe the whole surface or just the decoupage with the bags.

Age spots

Make instant coffee, using 2tbsp to a half cup of water. Again, cool without stirring. Pour most of the liquid away and flick some of the granules over the surface.

MOSAIC AND TIN

Mosaic tiles are commonly available in two forms – either in single colour batches mounted on a paper backing or in bags of assorted colours. You could substitute ceramic wall or floor tiles, or even pottery, but think twice before mixing them with mosaic tiles if you want a level surface, as for a table. It is possible to combine varying thicknesses, but it's a time-consuming business. You'll have to use ceramic tile adhesive, rather than PVA high bond, so you can vary the depth of the bed in which you lay them and check constantly with a spirit level.

Pure tin is not readily available, nor is it necessary for our technique. We used tin-plated steel for the French Dresser on page 70, a tougher material which you are unlikely to pierce. Some craft stores carry it, but builders' merchants may be the best local source. The alternative is a specialist metal supplier; check phone books for the nearest. Zinc is a substitute (see page 178) and is more generally available from builders' merchants. Tin and zinc are milled in various thicknesses (or gauges) so make sure your supplier understands how you intend to use them.

PUNCHING DESIGNS ON TIN

1 Use masking tape to secure the tin to a piece of chipboard and the traced design to the tin. Place the centre punch on one of the lines, hold upright and tap gently with the hammer.

2 Reposition the centre punch and continue working in the same way. Your aim is to dent the surface, not pierce it. The claw hammer could be replaced with a lighter pin hammer.

VARIATIONS
In these very typical motifs, large and small centre punches have been supplemented with the tip of a single-slot screwdriver. You can try varying the spaces between the holes too.

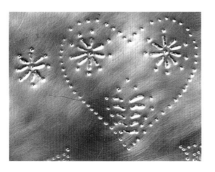

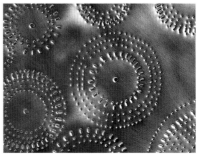

WORKING WITH MOSAIC TILES

MATERIALS
Sheets of mosaic tiles (or tesserae), mounted on brown paper; small, hand-fired ceramic wall tiles, a possible alternative; tile nippers with a spring-handled operation, much the easiest to use; a selection of assorted colours; ready-mixed grout (left) and ceramic tile adhesive, simpler to use than powdered varieties. Not shown: PVA high-bond adhesive and sealer – alternative adhesive

1 Once the basic outline has been drawn on the chosen surface, begin gluing the whole background tiles into position. Work from the corners and the outside edges inwards. Here, the ridged base of each tile was brushed with high-bond PVA adhesive and sealer.

2 Using the nippers, trim tiles to complete the background and glue into position. Then lay pieces to form the motif. I cut mine by hand but you can smash them (see page 176).

VARNISHES AND WAXES

The sealant or protective coat can affect the look of your makeover so profoundly that it's vital you choose the right product. When adapting our makeovers or designing your own, there several basic questions to ask yourself. Will the piece be used indoors or out? If outdoors, avoid waxes and go for yacht varnish. If indoors, how much protection do you want? Finishes in kitchens and bathrooms need a lot, as do those in children's rooms, where it's safest to opt for water-based products. Lastly, what is the final effect to be? Use matt varnish or wax (but don't buff) for a surface that feels natural. For a natural look, choose the low-sheen varnishes or waxes, bearing in mind that beeswax yellows and that tinted waxes (see Decoration) always alter the underlying colour as well as sealing, sometimes for an ageing effect, so run trials first. And remember there are times and places where it may be right to do without, as for the Bleached Wardrobe on page 51, where I wanted a 'raw' look.

PROTECTION

VARNISH TYPE	MEDIUM	HEAT RESISTANT	WATER RESISTANT	DURABILITY	SHEEN/ GLOSS	NON YELLOWING	PROJECT USED
Acrylic varnish *applied with brush* clear dead flat	ⓦ	✓	✓	▲	Low	✓	Metal Trunks – Verdigris and Gingham
clear matt	ⓦ	✓	✓	▲	None	✓	Wardrobe Shelving Fabric Bedheads – Moorish
clear satin	ⓦ	✓	✓	▲	Mid	✓	Wardrobe Doors – Gilded Drawers – Stencilled and Renaissance Gilded Table
Acrylic varnish *spray form* clear satin	ⓦ	✓	✓	◆	Mid	✓	Laminated Kitchen Units Dining Chairs – Metallic Loom Chairs
Lacquer varnish *spray form* clear gloss	⊙	✓	✓	◆	High	✓	Fridge-Freezer (see p.91)
Polyurethane varnish *applied with brush* clear matt	⊙	✓	✓	◆	None	✕	Café Tables (alternative for indoor use – see below)
Yacht varnish *applied with brush* clear matt	⊙	✓	✓	◆	None	✕	Café Tables (exterior use)

PROTECTION

WAX TYPE	MEDIUM	HEAT RESISTANT	WATER RESISTANT	DURABILITY	SHEEN/ GLOSS	NON YELLOWING	PROJECT USED
Acrylic varnishing wax *applied with brush or cloth* clear	(w)	✓	✓	◆	Mid	✓	Dining Chairs – Rush Seat and Fifties Retro Giverny Chair
Beeswax polish *applied with cloth*	(o)	✓	✓	▲	Mid	✕	French Dresser
Furniture wax or polish *applied with cloth* clear	(o)	✓	✓	▲	Mid	✓	Wardrobe Doors – Country French Dresser Console Tables Fabric Bedheads – Shaker
Transparent wax *applied with cloth* clear	(o)	✓	✓	▲	Mid	✓	Flexible Storage (casters) Four Poster

DECORATION

VARNISH TYPE	MEDIUM	HEAT RESISTANT	WATER RESISTANT	DURABILITY	METHOD
Crackle varnish *applied with brush*	(w)	✓	✓	▲	Apply between base and top coats to create a crazed, aged-paint effect.
Frosting varnish *applied with brush and roller*	(w)	✓	✓	◆	Apply to clear glass to reproduce the appearance of etching. Tint with colourizers.

WAX TYPE					
Acrylic varnishing wax *applied with brush or cloth*	(w)	✓	✓	◆	Tint with artists' acrylic colour to create an even, coloured stain/sealant. Buff for mid sheen.
Furniture wax or polish *applied with cloth*	(o)	✓	✓	▲	Tint with artists' oil colour to create an ageing, coloured polish/sealant. Buff for mid sheen. Also used for aged-paint resist technique (applied with small fitch).
Liming wax *applied with cloth*	(o)	✓	✓	▲	Apply to unpainted or painted wood to create soft, bleached effect as paste is retained in the grain when excess wiped off. Buff for mid sheen.

(w) = water-based
(o) = oil-based
▲ = suitable for average wear and tear (use in living room or bedroom)
◆ = suitable for heavy wear and tear (use in bathroom or kitchen)

FITTINGS

Never pass on a chance to sift through the handles, knobs and finials in any store. You don't have to spend a lot to find quirky fittings that can be the starting point for a makeover. The secret is not to think of them simply as finishing touches, and remember you can always paint, spray or decorate the fitting itself. I've tapped painted upholstery nails into painted wooden handles in a simple daisy motif to lift a simple set of drawers. If you want a traditional look, most DIY stores hold a basic range of shapes and there are specialist companies who offer more extensive selections.

Experiment with found objects too. Shells and driftwood, for example, can be used to great effect. Find the right shape and either could feature as designer pulls in a makeover for a bathroom cupboard. I'd use epoxy glue to mount the shell on a concealed dowel and screw that into position. I've also turned old dessertspoons into fun handles on a kitchen cabinet. Bend into a comfortable shape using pliers, drill a hole at either end and secure, using countersunk screws.

PREVIEW
Some of the most striking handles from our projects: 1 designer chrome, certainly the most expensive; 2 and 3 chain-store plastic, but sprayed silver; 4 more of the same, this time with a copper spray; 5 chrome handles teamed with traditional card holders – a surprising but successful combo

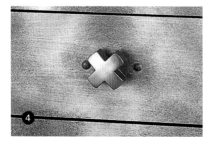

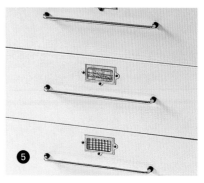

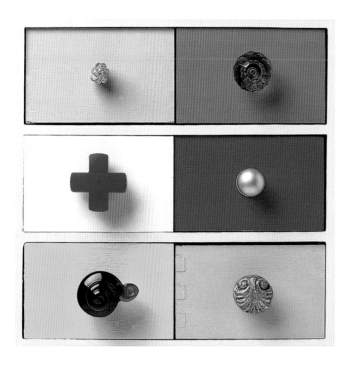

RAW MATERIALS
This unpainted set of drawers seemed the perfect way to demonstrate a few of the budget-range handles now on the market. Each one suggests various treatments. What about that red cross on the little run-about bedside table below?

FANCY FINIALS
We use them on a four poster, for tiebacks and for fabric bedheads. Wood, glass and metal – they are full of possibilities.

SIMPLE ADD-ONS
Add period legs or casters to this little bedside unit and it changes character instantly. The aged-paint finish survives its original makeover (see page 64), but the wild contrast here leaves me wanting to explore two very different looks.

PART TWO

FACELIFTS

Detailed step-by-step instructions for an inspiring and wide-ranging collection of makeovers for every room in your home, as well as ten pages of themed ideas for you to explore and develop for yourself

Bright, modern colours allied to some vigorous ageing techniques make a dramatic statement with this simple, rough, old coffer. I like the mixture of textures created by the heavy crackle glaze applied to the top (see page 148) and the dusty, rubbed-back look of the wax-resist aged paint effect on the panels below (see page 144).

ABOUT FACELIFTS

Treat this section as a portfolio of suggestions reflecting the range of basic furniture types, from storage, through tables and chairs to beds. Whether your style is country, fifties retro, chic minimalist or downright romantic, there's a makeover solution here for you. Each of our major projects is presented with step-by-step instructions for construction or adaptation (where appropriate) and decoration, cross-referred to our detailed techniques section in Part Three. So, if you were lucky enough to find a very similar piece, you'd have a complete guide to making our transformation for yourself, plus, in most instances, at least one alternative colourway. But that's not how we hope you'll use this book.

It's really a collection of mix and match options to co-ordinate in creating pieces that work for the way you live your life.

To take an example, let's imagine that your dream home boasts a perfectly adequate kitchen by the designer from hell.

For straightforward paint solutions, have a look at page 88 for our update on laminated units, or the copper effect on page 93 – another modern approach, but one that could accent a single cupboard in a run of colourwashed units too. For a stunning treatment that teams an aged paint technique with the simple crafts of punched tin and frosted glass, look at the French café look we've contrived for a junk-shop dresser with panelled doors (see page 70). We added a zinc top too – easy to fit following our instructions – but maybe not right for you.

If you're willing to try very simple adaptation, take another look at those kitchen doors. If they are flat, why not add a handsome moulding, and maybe change the handles on some doors and remove others completely, adding pretty fabric to the shelves and blinds or curtains at the open fronts? It would be easy enough to adapt our wardrobe shelving project on page 60, substituting for the shelf liners one of the PVC fabrics now available, and the gilded wardrobe project on page 52 can tell you all about fitting mouldings.

Left: This rustic cupboard with a Mediterranean feel is a clever assembly job prompted by the acquistion of some lovely old shutters. But look at the base – the drawer is set in a pretty flared and scalloped shape which could be jig sawed out to conceal much plainer legs. Woodwashes in tones of blue and green (see page 140) give it a sun-bleached look.

Opposite: There are several very interesting ideas to borrow here. Note the simple, effective use of Chinese characters (these could be hand painted or decoupaged – see page 160), the striking 'handles' (semi-circular sections cut and mounted on the door fronts), the tiny corner detail on the door panels and the steel pulls chosen to reflect the style of the piece.

If you're up for a little more simple DIY, there's the country-style wardrobe on page 54 – a very different approach to storage cupboards and another for flat doors. You could opt for single 'windows' and a natural look with the pale on paler colourway illustrated on page 151, plus inserts of cream on white gingham.

I've started and it's hard to stop, but I'm sure you'll have taken the point. Make time to look through all the projects – even those that don't seem relevant – so you know what can be achieved given some very rewarding time and effort.

Don't be put off by those which contain an element of construction. I am lucky enough to have a partner who translates my ideas into practice but I am confident that we have come up with pieces which combine good looks with achievable results. The methods are basic, the tools easy to use, and the skill level minimal. When we began, my confidence was low but I promise you that if I can do what's required, and I can, then anyone can. Those first nervous cuts with the jig saw are long behind me now. If you are inexperienced too, it makes sense to study the advice in Part One and work on your basic skills first. If the idea still fills you with dread, your local woodyard may be the answer. Most have staff who will cut wood to size and jig saw shapes to a template. Just be clear what you want before you go.

Kitsch glamour in a fun, fashionable interior which owes a lot to Hollywood in the thirties. Wooden inserts, strip moulding and corrugated iron transform some nondescript seating, while a mixture of metal leaf gilding and metallic paint (see page 168) put on the razzle dazzle. It's not furniture, I know, but I think the galvanized metal makeover on the old fireplace is a stunningly simple solution to a knotty problem.

Lastly, some practical advice. Read all the instructions, including cross-references, before you shop. Be aware that your measurements will almost inevitably differ from ours, and that this will affect the dimensions of materials like wood, metal and fabric, plus paint quantities. Be sure to adjust your shopping list accordingly.

WARDROBE DOORS

These three projects illustrate just how simple it is to give completely different identities to the same cupboard. The starting point: three new, ultra-basic, small wardrobes made of particle board with a white plastic finish. The result: a trio of stylish, free-standing cupboards that could easily claim a place other than the bedroom. The first, for example, makes a great linen cupboard or, if space allows, excellent bathroom storage, and the third would sit well in many cottage-style kitchens. But ideas like these can be adapted and applied equally well to those dauntingly bland ranks of fitted cupboards that many of us inherit, and are guaranteed to restyle any space in quite radical ways.

BLEACHED AND BATTERED

CLEANING AND PRIMING

Prepare the surface thoroughly by cleaning before and after construction; prime the doors (inside and out) and the exterior shell, as appropriate. See pages 12–17.

MATERIALS

Preparation ▶ 6mm (¼in) MDF or plywood, precut to size (see below)
Construction ▶ 200ml PVA wood glue / 12 panel pins / approx. 150 dome-headed upholstery nails / 20ml quick-dry epoxy glue
Base coat ▶ 500ml white vinyl matt emulsion
Wax resist ▶ 150ml furniture wax (clear)
Top coats ▶ 375ml white vinyl matt emulsion / 300ml turquoise artists' acrylic colour / 105ml monestial green artists' acrylic colour (2 coats)
Fittings ▶ 2 round mirrors (wood frame) / 2 nautical knobs and screws

EQUIPMENT

Screwdriver / metal rule / set square / ruler or straight edge / pencil / adjustable work bench (and/or G-clamps) / protective mask (if using MDF) / jig saw / medium- and fine-grade sandpaper / 2 x 25mm (1in) round fitches / pin or tack hammer / masking tape / scissors / drill with flat wood bit / mixing sticks / 2 x 50mm (2in) emulsion brushes / container to mix glaze / lint-free cotton rags / water to dampen rags

METHOD
Preparation

ALWAYS WEAR A MASK IF CUTTING MDF.
1 Remove the doors and knobs carefully, using the appropriate screwdriver. Reserve the hinges and their screws.
2 The simplest way to make the door frames is to cut each of them in one piece from wooden board and mount them on the existing doors. Use the metal rule, set square, ruler (or straight edge) and pencil to draw the outlines on both pieces of precut wood – the width of your frames will depend on your door and mirror sizes. With 36cm (14in) doors and 24.5cm (9½in) mirrors, we opted for frames 5cm (2in) wide.

3 Secure one piece of wood with clamps, cut out the central section, using the jig saw, and discard. Repeat for the second frame. Sand rough edges, using medium-grade sandpaper.

Construction

1 Using one of the fitches, apply a thin layer of PVA wood glue to one side of each frame and position on the outside of the doors.

2 Tap panel pins into each frame, one at each corner and one halfway down the long sides. Decorate with rows of upholstery nails.

3 Sand the mirror frames, back and front, with medium-grade sandpaper.

4 Decide the height of the mirrors and glue in place with epoxy glue, as the manufacturer's instructions.

5 Mask the glass with tape to protect from paint splashes. Tap upholstery nails round each frame.

6 Using the flat wood bit, drill random holes below the mirrors.

Aged paint finish

See page 144, Wax Resist. The battered, bleached look of the aqua on white doors entailed lots of sanding with fine-grade sandpaper and I omitted a sealant coat to enhance the effect.

Final assembly

Screw on the new handles and rehang the doors.

GILDED GLAMOUR

CLEANING AND PRIMING

Prepare the surface by cleaning before and after construction; prime the doors (inside and out) and the exterior shell. See pages 12–17.

MATERIALS

Preparation ▶ deep frame moulding, mitred to size (see opposite)
Construction ▶ 200ml PVA wood glue / approx. 24 panel pins
Base/top coats ▶ 375ml white vinyl matt emulsion / 300ml turquoise artists' acrylic colour /105ml monestial green artists' acrylic colour
Size coat ▶ 300ml italian water-based size
Gilding ▶ 30–40 loose sheets aluminium dutch metal leaf
Sealant coat ▶ 500ml satin acrylic varnish (clear)
Ageing glaze for moulding ▶ 150ml acrylic scumble glaze (transparent) / 150ml white vinyl matt emulsion / 100ml turquoise artists' acrylic colour / 5tsp monestial green artists' acrylic colour
Fittings ▶ 2 scroll handles with screws

EQUIPMENT

Screwdriver / graph paper / pencil / metal rule / ruler or straight edge / set square / 1 x 15mm (½in) round fitch / pin or tack hammer / 2 containers for mixing paint and glaze / mixing sticks / 2 x 50mm (2in) emulsion brushes / masking tape / scissors / lint-free cotton rags / 1 x 25mm (1in) flat bristle brush / disposable gloves / soft-bristled brush or clean duster / 1 x 50mm (2in) varnish brush

METHOD

Preparation

1 See Bleached Doors, Preparation, step 1, on page 50.

2 Mitring equipment is expensive to buy – although it can be hired – and difficult to use if you are inexperienced. Much the simplest solution is to get your chosen moulding mitred by your supplier. Picture-framing shops will sometimes do the work for you, but you will probably have to buy the timber elsewhere. (Clearly you need four short pieces and four long ones.) Whoever cuts the wood will need the final dimensions of the panels you want to create so measure your doors and decide where you want to place your moulding before you have it mitred. Draw a scale plan on graph paper to check fit. For maximum impact I chose a moulding with a very deep profile and set it 2.5cm (1in) from the edge of the door.

Construction

1 Mark the appropriate guide lines on each panel, using the pencil, ruler (or straight edge) and set square.

2 Brush a thin, even coat of glue onto the back of one of the short pieces, using the fitch, and position at the top of one door. Working clockwise, glue the remaining three pieces. Repeat for the other door.

3 Secure each length with evenly spaced panel pins tapped gently into the moulding with the hammer.

Base and top coats

1 Pour the white emulsion into one of the containers, add the turquoise and monestial green and stir well.

2 Apply two even coats to the prepared and primed surfaces with an emulsion brush, allowing 2–3 hours for each coat to dry.

WARDROBE DOORS

Gilding the moulding

See page 168 for the technique, omitting the base and sealant coats. I masked the surrounding areas with tape before applying the size, taking some of the tack off on clean rag first, and aimed for complete coverage when gilding, using fragments to patch.

Sealant coat

Stir the varnish well and apply to the doors, inside and out, and the shell, using the varnish brush. Allow to dry (2–3 hours).

Ageing the moulding

See page 147, Ageing with Glaze, for the technique. Remask the surrounding areas before you begin and quickly rub off the excess glaze with clean rags folded to form a pad. Allow to dry (1 hour) and remove the masking tape.

Final assembly

See Bleached Doors.

COUNTRY CHIC

CLEANING AND PRIMING

Prepare the surface by cleaning before and after construction; prime the doors (inside and out) and the exterior shell. See pages 12–17.

MATERIALS

Base coats ▶ 750ml premixed deep red vinyl matt emulsion (2 coats)
Glaze coat ▶ 250ml acrylic scumble glaze (transparent) / 3⅓tbsp burnt umber artists' acrylic colour
Sealant coat ▶ 200ml furniture wax (clear)
Fitting the mesh ▶ chicken wire / 50ml antique gold spray paint
Fitting the fabric ▶ approx. 2m x 140cm (2yd x 56in) tartan cotton / curtain wire, plus 16 eyes and hooks
Fittings ▶ 2 pre-patinated brass door knobs

EQUIPMENT

Screwdriver / metal rule / ruler or straight edge / set square / pencil / graph paper (optional) / adjustable work bench and/or G-clamps / jig saw / mixing sticks / 2 x 50mm (2in) emulsion brushes / container for mixing glaze / lint-free cotton rags / tin snips / newspaper to protect work surface / hand-held staple gun and appropriate staples / masking tape (optional) / bradawl / scissors / needle and thread

METHOD

Preparation

1 See Bleached Doors, Preparation, step 1.
2 Using the metal rule, ruler (or straight edge), set square and pencil, mark out the two openings for each door. Ours are the same size top and bottom – 22.5 x 99cm (9 x 39in) – but taller ones at the bottom look good too. It's wise to sketch designs to scale on graph paper before cutting.
3 Secure one of the doors with clamps, cut the upper and lower panels out carefully, using the jig saw, and discard. Repeat for the second door.

Dragging

See page 150 for the technique. Here the two premixed red emulsion base coats were dragged with a darker red mix. When applying glaze to the doors, aim for long strokes, working vertically on the long sides and horizontally on the 'cross members'.

Sealant coat

Using clean rags folded into a pad, apply the furniture wax, leave to set (15 minutes) and buff up with another clean rag.

Fitting the mesh

1 Using the tin snips, cut four sections of chicken wire to fit the openings in your doors, adding a 2.5cm (1in) allowance on all four sides.

2 Lay the pieces on the newspaper and, using a sweeping movement, spray one side only with antique gold, holding the can approx. 30.5cm (12in) from the surface. Allow to dry (1 hour).

3 Position on the reverse of the doors and staple into place at the top and bottom only, using horizontal rows of staples approx. 12mm (½in) from the edges. Secure the sides with masking tape while you work if you prefer.

Fitting the fabric

1 Using the tin snips, cut eight pieces of curtain wire, two for each opening, making all of them approx. 2.5cm (1in) shorter than the width of the openings. Screw an eyelet into either end of each piece.

2 Making the initial hole with the bradawl, screw a hook beside each corner of the mesh at every opening.

3 Cut out four pieces of fabric to match the openings, adding allowances of 5cm (2in) at the top and at the bottom of each piece and 10cm (4in) at each side. If you are afraid of fraying or simply must have neat edges, hem the sides before beginning step 4.

4 Using the needle and thread, turn the top and bottom edges of each piece to create a casing or open-ended hem for the wire, making sure all are wide enough for an eyelet to pass through them.

5 Thread the wires through the casings – the fabric gathers automatically – and hang the curtains. To the 'non-sewer' the last two steps may sound complicated. They really aren't – and this sort of fixing makes cleaning much simpler.

Final assembly

See Bleached Doors.

Another makeover for budget-range furniture, this small chest is also made of particle board. There's no adaptation involved – just a variety of painted surfaces and decorative effects and the replacement of some undistinguished wooden knobs. Indeed, for the first and the third it was the handles that dictated the treatment and the result is two very different pieces. If I have a favourite, it's the one below, but I had been looking for a way to use these chrome handles for ages. The second is interesting too. I was experimenting with ways of changing how we look at sets of drawers. A stencil that started life as a Ming vase turned almost Op Art in an attempt to assert a vertical view. It's an approach to adapt for a child's room, but do find a fun way to make the most of the knobs!

CONTEMPORARY GLOSS

CLEANING AND PRIMING

Remove the drawers and knobs and prepare the shell and drawer fronts thoroughly by cleaning (see pages 12–17) and priming with an oil-based primer (see page 142).

MATERIALS

Lacquer coats ▶ 1½ litres premixed bright yellow high-gloss paint (5 coats)
Fittings ▶ 3 aluminium card holders with screws / 3 long chrome handles with washers and nuts

EQUIPMENT

Mixing sticks / 2 x 50mm (2in) household brushes / wet and dry paper / lint-free cotton rags / warm soapy water / bradawl / drill with wood bits / screwdriver / pliers

METHOD
Lacquer effect

See page 142 for the technique. Do take the advice about appropriate surfaces seriously and study your piece of furniture objectively before you commit to this technique. Battered pieces are just not worth the effort. If you have any doubts, choose another paint finish.

Fittings

1 Decide the position of the card holders, use the bradawl and drill to make the required holes and then screw the holders into place.
2 Position the new handles, drilling the necessary holes for each on the inside of the drawers, and secure by tightening each external washer and internal nut with the pliers.

THREE WAYS WITH A SET OF DRAWERS

STENCILLED SIMPLICITY

CLEANING AND PRIMING	**Remove the drawers and knobs and prepare the shell and drawer fronts thoroughly by cleaning and priming. See pages 12–17.**
MATERIALS	**Base and top coats ▸ 500ml premixed bright yellow vinyl matt emulsion** **Stencils ▸ 380ml white vinyl matt emulsion / 120ml cobalt blue artists' acrylic colour** **Sealant coats ▸ 500ml clear satin acrylic varnish (2 coats)** **Fittings ▸ 6 wooden knobs**
EQUIPMENT	**Mixing sticks / 1 x 50mm (2in) emulsion brush / photocopier / A2 stencil card / masking tape / scissors / cutting mat / scalpel / lint-free cotton rag / 2 saucers / 2 x 25mm (1in) stencil brushes / 2 small, round artists' brushes / container for mixing paint / 1 x 50mm (2in) varnish brush / screwdriver**
METHOD **Base and top coats**	Stir the emulsion well and apply two even coats to the prepared and primed surfaces, allowing 2–3 hours for each coat to dry.

Stencilling

For the technique see page 159, Stippling; for the motifs, see page 182. First I stippled in the two vase shapes and then painted the primed new knobs with one of the artists' brushes, using 250ml white vinyl matt emulsion. I mixed the deep blue second colour in the container (using the remaining white emulsion and the cobalt blue), added the stripes with the second stencil, and painted parts of the knobs blue to complete the pattern. The stripe stencil was a useful guide here.

You need register marks to ensure the two stencils align correctly. See the motifs on page 182 for instructions.

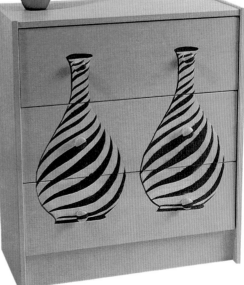

Sealant coats

Apply two coats of varnish, allowing 2–3 hours for each coat to dry.

Fittings

Screw the painted knobs in the same position as the original ones.

RENAISSANCE SPLENDOUR

CLEANING AND PRIMING

Remove the drawers and knobs and prepare the shell and drawer fronts thoroughly by cleaning and priming. See pages 12–17.

MATERIALS

Base coat ▶ 300ml white vinyl matt emulsion / 1tbsp dioxazine purple artists' acrylic colour
Glaze coats ▶ 400ml acrylic scumble glaze (transparent) / 1tbsp dioxazine purple artists' acrylic colour (3 coats)
Decoupage ▶ photocopies as required / 100ml purple water-based ink / 5tsp water (to dilute) / 200ml PVA adhesive or white glue
Gilding ▶ 200ml italian water-based size / approx. 3 loose sheets gold dutch metal leaf
Sealant coats ▶ 500ml clear satin acrylic varnish (2 coats)
Fittings ▶ 6 large brass door knobs

EQUIPMENT

Mixing sticks / 2 containers for mixing paint and glaze / 2 x 50mm (2in) emulsion brushes / water to dampen paper and cotton wool buds / small, round artists' brush / 2 saucers / cotton wool buds / sea sponge / newspaper / 1 x 25mm (1in) household brush / cotton rag / disposable gloves / 1 x 25mm (1in) flat bristle brush / 1 x 25mm (1in) soft-bristled brush or clean duster / 1 x 50mm (2in) varnish brush / screwdriver

METHOD
First and second dragging

For the technique see page 150. I used two coats of dark purple glaze over the paler purple base coat, reserving the final third for later. Both colours were mixed in containers and stirred well.

Decoupage

See page 161, Tinting with Water-based Inks, and basic recipe. The photocopies were tinted with a purple ink. (Ignore the base and sealant coats.)

Third dragging

Apply the third dragged coat, using reserved glaze.

Gilding

See page 168, Gilding with Metal Leaf, Size coat and Gilding only. I used small fragments of leaf, placing them randomly to give the effect of an immensely worn gilded surface.

Sealant coats and Fittings

See Stencilled Drawers. For a softer effect, use wax sealant.

WARDROBE SHELVING

This wardrobe was in a sad state when spotted in a junk shop. The shell was robust but the door was broken beyond repair. The thirties detail was too good to miss so I rescued it and decided to replace the door with a simple blind. Bright, gingham-lined shelves, crackle glaze in a modern colourway and hand-stamped decoration have created a cheerful and adaptable storage unit. Note the period headboard – this is a good shape which could easily be copied for a plainer cupboard.

CLEANING AND PRIMING

Prepare the surface thoroughly by cleaning before and after construction; prime inside, outside and shelves. See pages 12–17.

MATERIALS

Preparation ▶ 100ml fine ready-mixed wood filler / 6mm (¼in) MDF or plywood for new shelf, precut to required size (see below) / 12 x 19mm (½ x ¾in) battens for side and back / 19 x 87mm (¾ x 3½in) batten for front edge / ready-made decorative fretwork

Construction ▶ 150ml PVA wood glue / 15 screws / 50ml fine ready-mixed wood filler

Base coat ▶ 750ml premixed bright blue vinyl matt emulsion

Crackle coat ▶ 600ml acrylic crackle varnish (transparent)

Top coat ▶ 750ml premixed bright green vinyl matt emulsion

Sealant coats ▶ 1 litre clear matt acrylic varnish (2 coats)

Covering the shelves ▶ 4m x 140cm (4⅓yd x 56in) cotton gingham / 300ml fabric glue

Decorating the blind ▶ ready-made roller blind kit (size as required) / 150ml acrylic scumble glaze (transparent) / 150ml premixed bright blue vinyl matt emulsion / 3tbsp white vinyl matt emulsion / 3tbsp premixed bright green vinyl matt emulsion / plaster tassel / eyelet

Fitting the blind ▶ see kit / 50ml PVA wood glue / 4 panel pins

EQUIPMENT

Screwdriver / filler knife / medium-grade sandpaper / metal rule / adjustable work bench and/or G-clamps / tenon saw / drill with wood bits / 1 x 15mm (½in) round fitch / ruler or straight edge / spirit level / pencil / mixing sticks / 2 x 75mm (3in) emulsion brushes / 1 x 50mm (2in) household brush / 1 x 50mm (2in) varnish brush / iron / scissors / large plate / thick card to spread glue / lint-free cotton rags / junior hacksaw / container for mixing glaze / sea sponge / water to dampen and rinse sponge / 3 saucers / 2 x 35mm (1⅜in) diameter sponges for mini-roller / 2 small artists' brushes / bradawl / pliers

METHOD

Preparation

1 Remove the door hinges and the door.

2 Fill the hinge holes with ready-mixed wood filler (applied with the filler knife), allow to dry (1 hour) and sand.

3 Carefully unscrew the three supporting back and side battens for the original shelf and remove it. The pieces are to be used as a pattern for the second shelf.

4 Ask your local supplier to cut a piece of wood to size for the new shelf.

5 Measure the battens and, securing the timber with clamps, cut six new ones with the tenon saw – it's wise to replace those on the original shelf too.

6 In the same way and using the original shelf as a pattern, cut a batten for the underside of the front edge of the second shelf. A chunky shelf looks so much more generous than a thin one.

7 Measure the width of the opening and cut the piece of ready-made fretwork to fit, allowing a 2.5cm (1in) overlap for fixing on either side. Remember when choosing your design that it must be deep enough to conceal the blind mechanism. (You can cheat with extra beading, of course.)

Construction

1 Drill three equally spaced holes along the front edge of the second shelf.

2 Using the fitch, apply PVA wood glue sparingly to one of the narrow sides of the front-edge batten. Position carefully underneath the shelf, aligning it with the front edge. Clamp, secure with screws and allow to dry (1 hour).

3 Decide on the position of the two shelves, remembering that the front-edge battens make the shelves look deeper than they are. With the help of the tape measure, ruler (or straight edge) and spirit level, draw clear pencil guide lines for the position of the supporting battens both inside and outside the unit.

4 Drill two screw holes for each of the supporting battens.

5 Starting with the back battens and working from the outside, glue each one in place and secure with two screws. Allow to dry (1 hour). It's best to enlist someone's help here.

6 Fill all the drill holes with wood filler and allow to dry (1 hour). Rub down with the sandpaper.

Crackle finish

See page 148 for this technique, which was applied only to the outside of the wardrobe and one side of the fretwork. I used a premixed blue emulsion for the base coat, two coats of crackle varnish, and another premixed emulsion, in green, for the top coat. Although the green was brushed on vertically, the crackle effect was surprisingly variable. This is because the unit had been patch mended in the past and the various woods reacted differently.

Sealant coats

Stir the varnish well and, using the varnish brush, apply one or two coats to the crackle finish, allowing 2–3 hours for each coat to dry.

Covering the shelves

1 Iron the gingham. Trust me – don't skip this step. It makes the job much easier.

2 Lay one of the shelves face down on the gingham and use as a template to cut out a piece of fabric to cover, allowing a 2.5cm (1in) turning on the underside at the back and sides. Before you cut the fabric for the front edge, fold it up and over the batten to decide the correct allowance. Cut a second piece to match.

3 Measure the inside of the unit and cut out a series of manageable pieces to cover the sides, back, top and bottom, again allowing 2.5cm (1in) turnings along the edges. If it helps, draw a plan to remind you what fits where.

4 Pour a little of the fabric glue at a time onto the plate – it's much easier to quantity control like this. Using a small piece of thick card as a spreader, apply a thin, even coat to the tops of the shelves, their sides and to the undersides for the 2.5cm (1in) turnings.

5 Quickly put the fabric in place, overlapping, snipping carefully where required, and turning under for neatness. As it is thin and allows some glue to seep through, you should not need to add more. Smooth out any wrinkles with a clean rag before the glue dries.

6 To cover the inside of the unit, fit the top section(s) first, then the back, and finally those for the sides, repeating steps 4 and 5. Allow to dry (1 hour) before positioning the shelves.

Decorating the blind

1 If necessary, trim the blind to fit the opening. I had to shorten my roller and fabric by approx. 20cm (8in), using a junior hacksaw for the metal roller. Most kits include instructions on how to do the job – check yours does before you buy.

2 Pour the acrylic scumble glaze into the container, add the blue emulsion and stir well.

3 Unroll the blind and lay it flat, right side facing upwards, on a clean surface. See page 170, Glaze coat only, for how to apply the background colour.

4 See page 164 for the spot-stamping technique, using green on white emulsion, rather than artists' acrylics.

5 The plaster knob was also painted blue and green, using artists' brushes. To secure, I made a hole through the end batten and fabric (using a bradawl), screwed in the brass eyelet, and attached the knob using the kit hook, tightened with a pair of pliers.

Fixing the blind

1 Following the kit instructions, position the blind inside the opening so that it hangs in front of the shelves.

2 Using PVA wood glue and the fitch, glue the fretwork in place and secure with four panel pins.

ADAPTATION

Minimum tools/maximum imagination is the theme. Only the tall cupboard requires more than two tools – and, for the others, if your supplier will cut timber to fit you can do without a saw too. But it's the ways you adapt and rework these very basic ideas to suit your needs that make them valuable. Take the plate rack, for example. Forget plywood and fretwork and aim for a classical effect, adding top and side panels cut from architrave or creating a cornice from moulding. For the bathroom, try panels of driftwood. (See pages 42–3 for sealants.)

Left: We added legs and instant dignity to this squat bedside unit. It's amazing how often that simple trick works. Fake it with a few books to decide how long they should be. We used four tops for newel posts (available at large DIY stores), and each came fitted with a double-ended screw to attach it to the base. Colourway: white acrylic primer; aged paint finish – blue on white (see page 144). I highlighted the detail on the legs with bands of turquoise vinyl matt emulsion.

Left: Here basic shelving turns country plate rack with the addition of 6mm (¼in) plywood panels and fretwork edging, which is now available in many styles. All are secured with wood glue and panel pins. The shells were attached before I primed (see page 116). Colourway: white acrylic primer; crackle finish (see page 148) sides and front only – pink on yellow. I also dry brushed green emulsion on the yellow interior (to help it tone with the wall) and applied liming wax to the entire surface.

Left: A storage solution for the home worker who needs to integrate office and living space, this idea adapts the makeover on page 54. Two extra plywood shelves were added, supported on angle brackets, and the casters offer even more flexibility. But beware: it's vital to check your wardrobe base for stability before adding casters. Ours has a three-quarter section set back to create a plinth and requires a full-sized base to make it safe to move around – casters must be placed at the corners. It is also sensible to store heaviest items at the bottom. And note: with no curtains, the interior must be painted too. Colourway: white acrylic primer; exterior – water-based dragging (see page 150); interior – dragged glaze (250ml acrylic scumble, 2tbsp payne's grey and 1½tbsp titanium white artists' acrylics); casters – metal primer, dragged as exterior.

Above: Don't ditch the drawers when you dump a chest too damaged to restore. We removed the knobs (just for painting) and added small plywood shelves and dividers, secured with wood glue and panel pins. This, and the multi-coated finish, made a wall unit suitable for light storage in kitchen or bathroom. You could also mount two, end to end. See pages 27–8 for fixings. Colourway: lacquer finish – mid blue and yellow high-gloss paints (see page 142).

FLEXIBLE STORAGE
FOR HOME WORKERS

A pair of chunky modern casters, an easy paint technique and some elementary joinery turned this redundant pine blanket box into a hardworking piece of storage for a home worker desperate to keep documents and files separate from the everyday clutter of family life. It can be a chronic problem if you don't have the luxury of a room of your own and few of us want to solve it by importing traditional filing cabinets into our living spaces. One of the obvious joys of this solution is that its function is so easily concealed once work is over; the other is its mobility. Try lugging that filing cabinet into the next room to make way for a family gathering. I opted for two-colour woodwashing to preserve the grain and match the simple construction of this pine box. It is also an excellent technique for easing a new piece of furniture into an existing colour scheme. If your box is currently painted, you'll have to strip it first – or choose another finish.

CLEANING

Prepare the surface thoroughly by cleaning before and after construction. See pages 12–17. No priming is necessary.

MATERIALS

Preparation ▸ 6mm (¼in) steel rod / 25 x 25mm (1 x 1in) batten / 19mm x 1m (¾in x 3ft) rope
Construction ▸ 12 screws
First wash coat ▸ 210ml white vinyl matt emulsion / 4tbsp emerald green artists' acrylic colour / 1tbsp cadmium yellow artists' acrylic colour / 1tbsp pale olive green artists' acrylic colour / 175ml water
Second wash coat ▸ 270ml white vinyl matt emulsion / 2tbsp raw umber artists' acrylic colour / 175ml water
Base coat (bronzing) ▸ 4 trolley casters (10cm/4in wheels), plate fixing with appropriate screws / 100ml green acrylic spray paint
Size coat ▸ 3⅓tbsp italian water-based size
Bronzing ▸ 1tbsp copper bronzing powder
Protective coat (bronzing) ▸ 3⅓tbsp transparent polish (clear)
Final assembly ▸ 4 large ornamental studs (optional) / ½tbsp copper gilt cream

EQUIPMENT

Metal rule / adjustable work bench and/or G-clamps / junior hacksaw / masking tape (optional) / pencil / tenon saw / drill with wood and 6mm and 25mm (¼in and 1in) flat wood bits / medium-grade sandpaper / scissors / hanging file (to check fit) / screwdriver / 2 containers for washes / mixing sticks / 2 x 50mm (2in) emulsion brushes / lint-free cotton rags / large plate / disposable gloves / adjustable spanner / protective mask / dustsheet / 1 x 25mm (1in) flat bristle brush / small, flat artists' brush / small, soft-bristled brush / 1 x 25mm (1in) household brush / duster / pin or tack hammer (for optional studs)

METHOD

Preparation

1 Measure the internal width of the chest, secure the steel rod with clamps and cut two lengths to fit, using the junior hacksaw. These will form the supports for your hanging files. Ours were 33cm (13in) long. You can mark the rod with masking tape as a guide. (The keen-eyed may notice an extra batten in the front corner. We added it to strengthen a damaged batten inside the box.)

2 Measure the internal depth and, with the pencil, mark out four lengths on the batten. Clamp and cut, using the tenon saw. Again, ours were 33cm (13in) long.

3 Clamping each batten in turn, mark and drill a hole through it, approx. 2.5cm (1in) from one end – we'll call this the top – using the 6mm (¼in) flat wood bit.

4 Again clamping each batten in turn, substitute a standard wood bit and drill three equally spaced screw holes.

5 Use the pencil to mark the position of the two rope holes at each end of the chest and drill all four holes, using the 25mm (1in) flat wood bit. Our holes were approx. 11.5cm (4½in) apart and 10cm (4in) from the top of the chest. Smooth any rough edges with sandpaper.

6 Cut the rope in half, using the scissors.

FLEXIBLE STORAGE FOR HOME WORKERS

Construction

1 To assemble the supports for your hanging files, push each rod into the top holes on a pair of battens.

2 Place both pairs inside the box, with the rods uppermost, positioning one pair at one end with a batten in either corner. Use a hanging file to determine the correct positions for the other pair, adjusting the battens until the hooks at either side of the file hang on the rods. Mark the position of all four battens. We wanted to use foolscap folders so our rods were 39cm (15⅓in) apart.

3 Screw in the four battens, working from the inside.

Woodwashing

See page 140. I used two washes for the entire surface inside and out (excluding the bottom), the first green and the second a creamy white. The rope pieces were woodwashed green too. Wearing the disposable gloves, I poured a little of the wash onto the large plate and pressed a clean rag over it until it was saturated. Then, cupping the folded rag in one hand, I pulled the rope through it with a twisting action. Allow the standard drying time.

Bronzing the casters

PROTECT YOUR WORK SPACE WITH DUSTSHEETS BEFORE SPRAYING, WORK IN A WELL-VENTILATED AREA AND WEAR A MASK.

See page 169, Using Bronze Powders, for the technique. I decided to spray the green base coat rather than paint – it was so much easier to get even coverage. Remove the wheels, using the spanner, first.

Final assembly

1 Refit the wheels.

2 Turn the chest upside down and secure the casters at the four corners, using the fittings supplied and the spanner.

3 Knot one end of one piece of rope and, working from the inside, thread the other end out through one hole and in through its adjacent hole. Allowing enough slack for a handle, knot the free end on the inside and trim off the excess. Repeat for the other handle.

4 If using decorative studs, hammer one at each corner of the outside lid.

5 To highlight detail and texture, apply a little copper gilt cream to the rope and studs with a clean rag. Leave to set (approx. 15 minutes) and buff up with another clean rag.

FRENCH DRESSER

I found the bottom of this secondhand dresser first, and the top, when it turned up, was a perfect fit. Both were soundly made from chipboard covered in a wood laminate. The surfaces were finished with an oak stain/varnish also in excellent condition so preparation was limited to a good sanding. Although associated with country kitchens, free-standing kitchen units can be easily adapted, as here, for a less rustic feel. All the techniques I use can be adopted to revamp fitted units too.

CLEANING AND PRIMING

Prepare the surface thoroughly by cleaning; prime most exterior surfaces (including glass battens, if appropriate) but exclude lower door panels. See pages 12–17.

MATERIALS

Preparation ▶ 25ml silver metallic car spray paint
Base coat ▶ 330ml white vinyl matt emulsion / 3tbsp raw umber artists' acrylic colour
Wax resist ▶ 250ml furniture wax (clear)
Top coats ▶ 600ml white vinyl matt emulsion / 105ml monestial blue artists' acrylic colour / 3tbsp middle grey artists' acrylic colour (2 coats)
Sealant coat ▶ 350ml furniture wax (clear) or beeswax polish
Punching the tin ▶ tin-plated sheet steel for lower door panels / 100ml paint thinners / 100ml beeswax polish / 200ml strong-bonding, non-drip, multi-purpose contact adhesive / 8 brass-headed nails
Frosting the glass ▶ 150ml frosting varnish
Preparing the zinc ▶ sheet zinc for unit top
Fixing the zinc ▶ 125ml strong-bonding, non-drip, multi-purpose contact adhesive / approx. 30 copper roofing nails
Refitting ▶ approx. 8 panel pins / 2 chrome door handles / 2 chrome drawer pulls / screws (if not supplied) / small dowels (if required)

EQUIPMENT

Screwdriver / small chisel (if required, to remove putty) / newspaper to wrap glass and for template / marker pen / metal rule / 2 containers for mixing paint / mixing sticks / 2 x 50mm (2in) emulsion brushes / 2 x 25mm (1in) round fitches / fine- and medium-grade sandpaper / lint-free cotton rags / water to dampen rags / ruler or straight edge / pencil / 2.5cm (1in) masking tape / Chinagraph pencil / tin snips / rubber mallet / 15mm (½in) chipboard, approx. 30 x 60cm (1 x 2ft) / photocopier / 2 sheets A2 tracing paper / centre or nail punch / pin or tack hammer / cotton gloves / wet and dry paper / bradawl or drill with metal bit / gaffer tape (for unfitted glass) / scissors / window cleaner / 2 sheets A4 matt transfer film / cutting mat / scalpel / large plate / 1 x 25mm (1in) household brush / 1 x 100mm (4in) sponge mini-roller / permanent pen / tile cutter / bolster chisel / claw hammer / 50 x 50mm (2 x 2in) batten (to shape zinc), approx. 30cm (12in) long / protective mask / pliers / coarse wirewool

FRENCH DRESSER

METHOD
Preparation

1 Remove all the handles, knobs and hinges, using the screwdriver. Store the handles, knobs and screws for possible future use. Spray the hinges with two coats of silver metallic paint, allowing 1 hour for each coat to dry, and set them aside for refitting later.

2 Using the tip of the screwdriver, very carefully loosen the panel pins in the battens which support the glass, and take out both pieces. A small chisel is a great help if you have to remove old putty – but be gentle.

3 Wrap sound glass in several sheets of newspaper and label clearly with the marker. Take measurements for new glass, if required. Set the battens aside for painting.

Aged paint finish

See page 144 for the technique. I applied the ice blue top coats over a creamy white. If you want a subtly aged effect (as here), apply the wax resist sparingly – just to the door edges and mouldings.

Sealant coat

Using clean rags folded into a pad, apply the furniture wax (or beeswax polish), leave to set (15 minutes) and buff up.

Punching the tin

See page 177 for the technique; for the motifs, page 182. Our door panels each measured approx. 30.5 x 62cm (1 x 2ft). I added a line to follow the shape of each panel. To do the same, use a ruler to draw a line approx. 12mm (½in) from the edge of the tracing once you have transferred the motifs. Punch the marks for the decorative lines 1cm (⅜in) apart, but leave smaller gaps (approx. 5mm/⅛in) when forming letters.

Frosting the glass

See page 180 for the technique and page 182 for the motif. Our glass panels were 28 x 46cm (11 x 18in). I used 2.5cm (1in) masking tape for the stripes above and below each cup but they might look even better if I had used a narrower tape. Remember to reverse one of the cups when tracing the motifs so that both handles will face inwards.

Preparing the zinc

1 Using the metal rule, ruler (or straight edge) and marker pen, make a pattern for the dresser worktop out of newspaper, adding allowances for all four edges and turn-unders at front and sides as shown on the sketch on page 182. Our top measured 44 x 85cm (17⅓ x 33½in).

2 Stick your pattern to the wrong side of the zinc sheet with masking tape, draw round the basic outline with the permanent pen, and cut out, using the tin snips.

3 Again using the ruler, metal rule and permanent pen, carefully transfer all the fold and cut lines from your pattern to the zinc. Accuracy will make folding much easier.

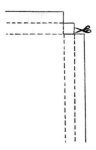

4 Using the tin snips, make the small corner cut as shown in the diagram. This separates the turn-unders at the front from those at the side. Snip the other three corners in the same way.

5 Flatten the cut edges and protect with masking tape.

6 See Shaping and Bending a Zinc Sheet on page 25, step 1, line 5 onwards, for the technique. The initial shaping (scoring and then marking with the bolster chisel) is carried out on the reverse side of the zinc. Turn the sheet over and position on the unit before you start to bend the fold at the back, and the inner folds at the sides and front. Although this may seem an unnecessarily complicated process, that piece of batten is important. If you hammer a zinc surface directly, you will mark it. You'll also find the batten helps you to spread the pressure as you work on the folds.

Fixing the zinc

1 Remove the zinc and, using medium-grade sandpaper, sand the unit top and the corresponding reverse section of the zinc. Wipe both clean with damp rag and leave to dry.

2 Put on the protective mask, stir the glue well and apply evenly to both surfaces with the fitch used to glue the tin.

3 Reposition the zinc on the unit top and smooth the glued surface down, using the batten and hammer. (It takes approx. 25 minutes for the glue to dry.)

4 Working with the hammer and wood as before, continue shaping the back, front and sides. Bend the outer sections at the sides and front under the overhangs.

5 To finish the corners, use the pliers to fold each corner tab in half diagonally, bending the top corner downwards and backwards (see Fig 1). Then, using the hammer and wood again, bend each triangular tab round its corner to the side. Hammer very gently to avoid creating sharp edges here.

6 Make a pilot hole with the bradawl or metal bit and secure each tab with a copper nail (see Fig 2). Four will secure the top but, if (like me) you want to feature the nails, tap in all round, spacing them evenly. These nails have long shafts so shorten them with the tin snips first.

7 Using the coarse wirewool and a circular action, rub the top down to improve the texture of the zinc – it is often sold covered with a waxy film. Wipe clean with damp rag.

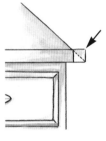

Fig 1 Front view

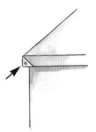

Fig 2 Side view

Refitting

1 Slot the glass back into the door panels and replace the battens, securing with panel pins.

2 Screw the resprayed hinges back onto the unit, and rehang all the doors, using the original screws.

3 Attach the new handles and drawer pulls, checking first that the original holes in the wood are the correct size for the screws supplied with the new fittings. If they are too small, use the bradawl or drill to enlarge them slightly. If too large, plug the holes with small dowels to fit.

4 Position the upper section carefully on top of the base.

GILDED TABLE

Circular one-piece and gate-leg dining tables are so commonplace in the secondhand shops I haunt it's easy to overlook them. But some offer such excellent value to anyone furnishing a first home away from home that it seemed feeble to resist the challenge they represent. Here, then, I concentrate on the cheaper end of the spectrum, avoiding hardwoods like oak and mahogany which are best simply restored, and suggest one way of creating interest on a neglected space – the table top. It's an idea that could be adapted for tables of any shape and size.

GILDED TABLE

CLEANING AND PRIMING

Prepare the surface thoroughly by cleaning and priming as appropriate. See pages 12–17.

MATERIALS

Base coat ▶ 700ml white vinyl matt emulsion / 300ml monestial blue acrylic artists' colour
Gilding base coat ▶ 350ml premixed deep blue vinyl matt emulsion
Size coat ▶ 350ml italian water-based size
Gilding ▶ 40 loose sheets gold dutch metal leaf
Sealant coats ▶ 1 litre clear satin acrylic varnish (2 coats)

EQUIPMENT

Container for mixing paint / mixing sticks / 2 x 50mm (2in) emulsion brushes / pencil / ruler or straight edge / set square / metal rule / small nail / pin or tack hammer / newspaper and scissors for pattern (if required, see below) / approx. 1m (1yd) string / graph paper / plastic ruler and masking tape (optional) / disposable gloves / 1 x 25mm (1in) flat bristle brush / 1 x 25mm (1in) round, very soft-bristled brush or clean duster / 1 x 50mm (2in) varnish brush

METHOD
Base coat

1 Pour the emulsion into the container. Add the monestial blue and stir well.

2 Apply two even coats to the entire table with one of the emulsion brushes. Allow 2–3 hours for each coat to dry.

Drawing the chequer board

1 To find the centre of your table, follow steps 2–3 or 4–5.

2 If it is a drop-leaf table, lower the flaps to form two straight sides. Using the pencil, ruler (or straight edge) and set square, draw a line down each of the other two sides to complete a rectangle. Mark the halfway point on each long side and rule a line between them.

3 Mark the halfway point of that line and you have found the centre. Tap the nail lightly into the centre point and raise the table flaps. Ignore steps 4–5.

4 If it is not a drop-leaf table, tape several sheets of newspaper together, place the table upside down on them and draw round its circumference with the pencil. Cut out the resulting pattern, fold into quarters and you have the centre point.

5 Unfold the pattern, lay it on the table (right side up!), tap the nail lightly into the centre and remove the pattern.

6 Once your nail is in position, tie one end of the string to it to form the 'fixed arm' of your improvised compass. Draw the string taut and experiment to decide the size of your circle. Mine had a diameter of 107.5cm (42½in). Trim the string, if necessary, and tie the pencil to the free end, making allowance for the knot. Carefully draw your circle.

7 Use the set square and ruler to divide the circle into quarters, taking the line drawn through the centre point as a guide. (If you used a pattern to find your centre point, you need to draw this line first.) Then measure and draw a grid of equally spaced vertical and horizontal lines to create your chequer board. Mine was based on a 12.5cm (5in) square – convenient because dutch metal leaves are this size – but rule your design out to scale on graph paper to check fit.

Gilding

For the technique, see page 168, including the Sealant coat. Gilding was applied to alternate squares of the chequer board and the edge of the table on a base coat of deep blue. Use a plastic rule (bevelled side down) as a guide if you are worried about painting straight lines. It's your choice how much of the base coat shows, but subtlety works best.

Sealant coats

Stir the varnish well and apply one or two coats to the entire table. Allow 2–3 hours for each coat to dry.

MASKING

This simple effect can add instant interest to any flat or textured surface. All you need is a quantity of flat shapes to mask the chosen areas. Try, as I did, looking for ready-made masks. Experiment is the keyword – with colours as well as shapes. You may choose to work with natural forms but that's no reason to limit yourself to nature's tints. To secure your mask, spray a thin coat of spray mount on the reverse (except for ferns, see below) and press firmly into position. For the spray technique, see page 99. Cover the entire surface, including the masks, for an even finish but avoid soaking paper. Peel off gently before the paint begins to dry. (See pages 42–3 for sealants.)

Below: Falling plane leaves inspired this effect, although I've never seen them so well behaved. I used more than fifty gathered in a local park – often a good hunting ground. Press in thick books first. Colourway: primer and base coat – see page 52; top coat – burgundy acrylic spray paint. Less formal patterns look good too.

Above: Simple motifs with bold colour contrasts work best for well-defined images, and a smooth surface may also sharpen an image. But opt for toning colour or the smudgy effect of spraying through complex patterns and the results are often delightful, as here. Colourway: white acrylic spray primer; base coat – oatmeal acrylic spray paint; top coat – deep blue acrylic spray paint. Masking with lace can also be effective on very smooth surfaces.

Some green ferns make wonderful masks. I begged mine from a friend, but florists sometimes hold a stock. Press and place face down – the underside is often dotted with tiny, dusty spores. It's wise to brush your surface before spraying too.

Colourway: white acrylic spray primer; base coat – salmon pink acrylic spray paint; top coat – as cupboard opposite.

KITCHEN TABLE
TO CONSOLE TABLES

This cunning plan is the kind of project that really pleases me. The end result is a handsome pair of narrow tables that would stand happily in a long hallway, in the alcoves on either side of a fireplace (instead of the ubiquitous bookshelves), or flanking a tall window. But they started life as one very plain, rectangular kitchen table topped with a laminate that was beginning to lift off. Don't let the construction deter you – it's pretty basic and you can always enlist someone else's help if you prefer. My design and decoration were inspired at least in part by the Gothick Revival, though it's easy enough to reshape the backplate and leg insets to some very different style. Remember too that if you are content with just one table this could be the ideal solution for some knocked-down reject with a damaged leg.

CLEANING AND PRIMING

Prepare the surface thoroughly by cleaning before and after construction and by priming. See pages 12–17.

MATERIALS

Preparation ▶ 9mm (⅜in) MDF or plywood
Construction ▶ 12 screws / 19 x 19mm (¾ x ¾in) quadrant batten / 50ml PVA wood glue / 40 panel pins / 12 x 12mm (½ x ½in) batten
Base coat ▶ 440ml white vinyl matt emulsion / 2tbsp raw umber artists' acrylic colour / 2tbsp burnt umber artists' acrylic colour
Wax resist ▶ 100ml furniture wax (clear)
Top coat ▶ 500ml premixed deep orange-red vinyl matt emulsion (1 coat only)
Ageing glaze ▶ 150ml acrylic scumble glaze (transparent) / 1tbsp premixed deep orange-red vinyl matt emulsion / ½tbsp burnt umber artists' acrylic colour
Decoupage ▶ photocopies as required / 100ml green water-based ink / 5tsp water (to dilute) / 50ml PVA adhesive or white glue /
Ageing wax ▶ 150ml furniture wax (clear) / 1tsp raw sienna artists' oil colour
Fixing ▶ screws and wall fixings (see pages 27–8)

EQUIPMENT

Pencil / ruler or straight edge / set square / adjustable work bench and/or G-clamps / protective mask (if using MDF) / jig saw / medium- and fine-grade sandpaper / metal rule / photocopier / A2 paper / scissors / drill with wood and masonry bits / screwdriver / tenon saw / 1 x 15mm (½in) round fitch / pin or tack hammer / 2 containers for mixing paint and glaze / mixing sticks / 3 x 50mm (2in) emulsion brushes / 1 x 25mm (1in) round fitch / lint-free cotton rags / water to dampen rags, paper and cotton buds / small artists' brush / 3 saucers / cotton-wool buds / sea sponge / newspaper to protect work surface / 1 x 25mm (1in) household brush

KITCHEN TABLE TO CONSOLE TABLES

METHOD

Preparation

ALWAYS WEAR A MASK IF CUTTING MDF.

1 Mark the cut line clearly across the table top, using the pencil, ruler (or straight edge) and set square. Our table was divided in half to make two pieces 29.5cm (11⅜in) deep and

91cm (35⅝in) wide. If the table you plan to use is larger, or you want narrower consoles, you may need to draw two cut lines to the appropriate depth. (The central section will be thrown away once the table is cut.)

2 Secure the table with G-clamps to keep it steady and cut along the pencil line with the jig saw. Rub the cut edges with sandpaper until they are smooth.

3 Measure the width (or cut edge) of one of the table tops and, using a photocopier and sheets of A2 paper, enlarge the template for the backplate on page 183 to fit. Enlarge the template for the leg insets to the appropriate size.

4 Cut out the full-sized templates and check the backplate against your table. You may need to adapt the lower section to secure it to your base. Now is also the time to consider making adjustments to the upper section. You can use newspaper to patch the existing template or even recut it to create a different profile. Hold your revised template in position to check its proportions.

5 Once you are happy with the backplate, lay the templates on the wood – we used a piece of MDF approx. 1 x 1m (39 x 39in) – and draw a clear line round them. You need two backplates and four leg insets for a pair of tables.

6 Clamp the wood securely and cut out the pieces, using the jig saw. Smooth the cut edges with sandpaper.

Construction

1 Turn one table to lie cut edge upwards and ask someone to hold one of the backplates in place, while you mark with the pencil the position of the six screws which will join it to the table. You need four along the cut edge of the table top and one below at each side to secure it to the base.

2 With the backplate still held firmly in position, drill the six screw holes, making sure the drill passes through the backplate and into the table.

3 Using the screwdriver, join the backplate to the table.

4 Turn the table over and, using the tenon saw, cut a piece of quadrant batten to the width of the table. This will finish the join between the table top and backplate.

5 Using the small fitch, brush a narrow strip of PVA wood glue onto the table top where the batten will sit. Position the batten and secure by tapping in four panel pins, using the pin hammer.

6 Turn the table upside down and place one of the leg insets in position. Tap a panel pin into the table base and another into the leg to secure it temporarily. Repeat for the other leg.

7 To support and strengthen the insets, cut four pieces of square batten to match the straight sides of the design – we needed two long and two short ones, in total approx. 1m (3ft).

8 Using a pair of pieces for each inset, glue the battens to the inside of the inset, table base and leg. Tap three panel pins into each piece to secure. (We decided to tap the panel pins part way into the battens before brushing on the glue. There was less risk of disturbing the insets when securing them.) Allow all glued areas to dry before painting (1 hour).

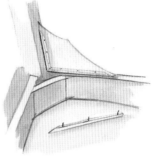

9 Repeat steps 1–8 to assemble the other table.

Aged paint finishes	See page 144, Wax-Resist method, and page 147, Ageing with Glaze. I used a specially mixed cream base coat under a single premixed deep orange-red vinyl matt emulsion top coat for the resist technique. The burnt umber in the ageing glaze darkens the red top coat to add a convincing patina. I delayed a sealant coat (Ageing wax, below) until I had added the decoupage.
Decoupage	See page 161, Tinting with Water-based Inks, and the basic recipe. I coloured all the photocopies with a diluted green ink. (Ignore the base and sealant coats.)
Ageing wax	See page 146. Tinted with raw sienna, this gives a softer, aged look to the decoupage and paint finish.
Fixing to the wall	Fit the masonry bit to the drill and ask someone to hold each table in position while you drill two holes through the lower section of the backplate and into the wall. Secure as appropriate (see pages 27–8).

CAFE TABLES

The simple design of the café table is a classic but if the one you have is a little battered, you fancy a change, or just want to jazz up your garden with a new look for a long-running standard, any of these ideas will work well. Each one offers a resilient finish suitable for outdoor use but each is also attractive enough for a conversatory or garden room and for other informal indoor uses. Just substitute two coats of polyurethane varnish for the yacht varnish mentioned on pages 86–7.

Although I concentrate on the table top here, the legs can also be decorated in a variety of finishes, such as verdigris, gilding or bronzing (see pages 166–9), and you could decorate the accompanying chairs with a similar or complementary finish for a stunning addition to your garden. If you want to try but don't have a metal café table, check out the large chain stores for inexpensive copies – a cheaper and better option than chasing the limited supply of secondhand originals. You can adapt these ideas for wooden or plastic laminate table tops too. Or, on a grander scale for high days and holidays, have a much larger circle cut from chipboard and support it on a couple of inexpensive trestles.

MOSAIC TABLE TOP

CLEANING/PRIMING

Prepare the surface by cleaning and priming. See pages 12–17.

MATERIALS

Preparation ▸ tiles (all 19 x 19mm/ ¾ x ¾in) – approx. 225 pale blue / 225 pale green / 450 ultramarine / 150 orange / 150 red / 150 yellow / 100 black / 100 assorted gold and turquoise
Fixing the tiles ▸ 500ml high-bond PVA adhesive and sealer
Grouting the tiles ▸ 500ml ceramic tile grout
Tinting the grout ▸ 2tsp pale olive green artists' acrylic colour / 1tsp titanium white artists' acrylic colour / 5tsp water

EQUIPMENT

See page 174, omitting ruler and photocopier and adding compass with extendable arm

METHOD

See page 174. There's no need to buy a compass. Just improvise by drawing round several plates to create the circles which are the basis of this essentially simple design. You can vary the sizes, but remember any changes you make will have an effect on colour numbers. I laid the tiles approx. 2–3mm (¹⁄₁₆–⅛in) apart.

STAMPED TABLE TOP

CLEANING/PRIMING   Prepare the surface by cleaning and priming. See pages 12–17.

MATERIALS   Base coat (outer circle) ▶ 300ml deep yellow vinyl matt emulsion
Top coat (outer circle) ▶ 4tsp cadmium yellow artists' acrylic colour /
2tsp titanium white artists' acrylic colour
Base coat (inner circle) ▶ 150ml white vinyl matt emulsion / 125ml cobalt
blue artists' acrylic colour / 5tsp emerald green artists' acrylic colour
Top coat (inner circle) ▶ 5tsp permanent light blue (phthalocyanine blue)
artists' acrylic colour
Stamping the spots ▶ 8tbsp titanium white artists' acrylic colour /
4tbsp permanent light blue (phthalocyanine blue) artists' acrylic colour /
4tbsp brilliant yellow green artists' acrylic colour
Sealant coats ▶ 750ml clear matt yacht varnish (3 coats)

EQUIPMENT   Compass with extendable arm or large plate / pencil / ruler / 1 sheet A2
matt transfer film / scalpel / cutting mat / 2 x 38mm (1½in) emulsion
brushes / 5 saucers / 2 x 50mm (2in) emulsion brushes / 3 x 35mm (1⅜in)
diameter sponges for mini-roller / 1 x 50mm (2in) varnish brush

METHOD   See page 31 for how to use transfer film. Draw a circle with a
diameter of 27cm (10½in) on the film and cut it out, keeping
both pieces. Mask the centre of the table with the circle and
apply the base coat to the outer circle, allowing to dry (2–3
hours). Dip just the brush tip into the top coat colour-mix to
dry brush the outer circle. Repeat for the inner circle, using
the other mask. See page 164 for stamping.

LAPIS LAZULI TABLE TOP

For a straight take on the technique shown on page 154 just double the quantities given. Equipment and Method are as there. But hold the fitch 20–30cm (8–12in) from the surface while you spatter and don't forget to prepare the surface first (see pages 12–17). For sealant coats, see opposite.

DECOUPAGE TABLE TOP

See page 161, Tinting with Water-based Inks, for the technique. I used 150ml bright green ink to tint the paper. The base coat (500ml white vinyl matt emulsion mixed with 3½tbsp dioxazine purple artists' acrylic colour) was dry brushed (see opposite) with a mix of 150ml acrylic scumble glaze and 2tsp dioxazine purple. For Cleaning and Priming, see pages 12–17. For sealant coats, see opposite.

LAMINATED KITCHEN UNITS

There's no need to despair of dragging those old kitchen units into the twenty-first century. Spray paint and judicious restyling of knobs and pulls will render the ugliest laminated or melamine-coated fittings unrecognizable. I've used metallic colours for a space-age look but the range is considerable. Try them on test boards before committing to a scheme.

CLEANING AND PRIMING

Prepare the surface thoroughly by cleaning; prime with white acrylic spray primer. See pages 12–17; see also page 99 for spray technique.

MATERIALS

Preparation ▶ 25mm (1in) plywood for worktop, precut to size (see page 90)
Shells, drawer fronts and doors ▶ (for base unit: 88 x 106cm/34½ x 42in and upper unit: 71.5 x 97cm/28 x 38in) 300ml copper metallic car spray paint / 400ml deep purple acrylic spray paint / 400ml mint green acrylic spray paint / 300ml pale blue metallic car spray paint / 150ml peach metallic car spray paint
Sealant coats ▶ 1.2 litres clear satin acrylic spray varnish (2 coats)
Final assembly ▶ 2.5cm (1in) self-adhesive, ridged chrome trim / 6 chrome knobs with appropriate screws

EQUIPMENT

Screwdriver / metal rule / dustsheets / 1 x 10cm (4in) roll brown-paper adhesive masking / scissors / protective mask / 4 sheets A3 matt transfer film / compass with extendable arm or large plate or similar / pencil / cutting mat / scalpel / set square / ruler or straight edge / knife with rounded handle / drill with wood bit (if required, see below)

METHOD
Preparation

PROTECT YOUR WORK SPACE WITH PLASTIC DUSTSHEETS BEFORE SPRAYING, WORK IN A WELL-VENTILATED AREA AND WEAR A MASK.

1 Take out the drawers and use an appropriate screwdriver to remove all the doors. Store the screws – you will need them again.

2 Remove any handles. This is worth doing even if you plan to reuse yours – it's so much easier to achieve good, even coverage when spraying without them.

3 Carefully remove the worktop from the base unit, noting how and where it is attached. Store the brackets and screws for later use.

4 Measure the length and width of the worktop before disposing of it. Ask your supplier to cut the new plywood top to the appropriate size. Ours was 107 x 53cm (42 x 20¾in).

Spraying the unit shells and drawers

With the same spray technique (see Priming) and brown-paper masks to prevent overspill, use copper for the plinth and purple for the remainder of the base unit, spraying the outside only. See page 31 for the masking technique. No masking is needed when spraying the upper unit mint green or the drawers copper, again outsides only.

Spraying the upper doors

1 For the outside of the left-hand door, use self-adhesive matt transfer film to prevent overspill when spraying the circle blue and the remainder of the door peach. See page 31 for the masking technique. If you don't already own an extendable compass, don't buy one specially. The easiest and very cheapest solution must be to improvise with a large plate or even a cookie tin of the right diameter. Place it on the matt transfer film, just draw round it with the bold pencil and your

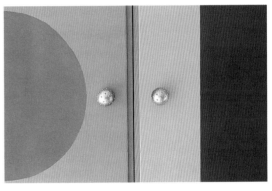

problem is solved. My circle had a 34cm (13⅜in) diameter.

2 For the outside of the right-hand door, mask with brown paper to spray a copper rectangle and mint green frame. My rectangle was approx. 25.5 x 45.5cm (10 x 18in).

Spraying the base doors

1 For the outside of the left-hand door, use two strips of evenly spaced 10cm (4in) brown-paper masking to spray alternate stripes of mint green and copper. Check the positions of the tape with the metal rule, ruler (or straight edge) and set square before spraying.

2 For the outside of the right-hand door, see Spraying the upper doors, step 1 – but reverse the colours, making the circle peach this time.

Sealant coats

Shake the varnish well and apply two coats to all the sprayed surfaces and to the worktop, allowing 1 hour between coats and 2–3 hours for the second coat to dry.

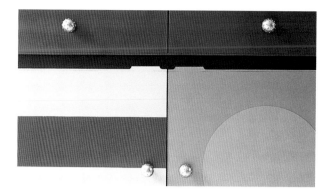

Final assembly

1 Position the varnished worktop and secure in the same way as before, using all the original brackets and screws.

2 To add the chrome trim, measure the edges you want to cover – it may only be the front edge if you have several units side by side – and cut the required length(s), using the scissors. I decided to cover the front and both sides of ours.

3 Peel off the backing and press the tape into position, smoothing it with the handle of the knife. Work on small sections at a time. See the illustration on page 21.

4 Where necessary, drill a screw hole for the new handle in each of the doors and attach, using the screws provided. Repeat for the drawers.

5 Replace doors, using original screws.

SPRAYING FRIDGES AND FREEZERS

You can use the same spraying and masking techniques to brighten these dreary monoliths too. So here are just a few, probably unnecessary, reminders. Empty, disconnect and defrost (if necessary) before you begin! Wash down with a sugar soap solution. Use masking tape and/or brown-paper masking to protect all switches, knobs, door handles and seals. Don't attempt to remove the handles or spray the 'working' parts at the back. Handles make it more difficult to achieve a smooth finish but you are likely to damage the machine if you take them off. Keep the door(s) closed while spraying; open to dry.

For this fridge-freezer (which was 58.5 x 183cm/23 x 72in), I primed with 800ml grey acrylic spray primer, decorated with 1.2 litres silver acrylic spray paint and 400ml blue metallic car spray paint, and added a sealant coat of clear lacquer spray (400ml), allowing 1–2 hours for that to dry.

METAL

The real fun of using paint finishes that look like metal is the element of surprise you can introduce to almost any interior. The kitchen cabinet apparently fashioned of beaten copper and the verdigris chair both come into that category, and I have seen a stunning metal effect on a sixties sideboard. Simple forms – hard-edged shapes that could be made of metal – will almost always help you create convincing results and this might be the solution if you are tired of the sleek, matt black laminate look that dominated eighties interiors. Verdigris and copper effects can also work well with more rounded, wrought forms. The traditional bentwood chair is one obvious example – cheap copies are not hard to find. You can use these finishes on real metal too, of course, and with new filing cabinets so expensive this is a great way of brightening old equipment for a home office. See page 166 for the paint techniques and pages 42–3 for sealants. The 'studs' mentioned in the captions are upholstery nails, tapped in before priming.

Pewter for a bedside cabinet: the slightly pitted surface of black laminate on chipboard took spray paint well and contributed to the final result. This is the low-key partner in my trio of metal effects so I opted for funky new handles (made of plastic) and sprayed them copper. Note the discreet stud on each side.

Right: A copper effect gives this tired kitchen cabinet a space-age feel. Studs, placed approx. 7.5cm (3in) apart, frame the doors and inscribe two centred circles. The dark halo effect was pure serendipity. One coat of primer had failed to hide an earlier paint finish but I liked the look so much that I emphasized it when applying the glaze. New plastic handles sprayed silver add that final lift.

Left: This chain-store chair is almost medieval given a verdigris finish. I wish I'd used studs on the legs too – just a pair on each side of the verticals where they meet the horizontals. But if you choose the right setting, the effect will still convince. A single chair in a hallway could look great – and those with a sense of drama might try a sombre set around a plain, long table.

NO-SEW COVER
FOR AN OLD SOFA

Whether you've changed your colour scheme, inherited some cast-off or just got bored with a one-time favourite, re-upholstery may be beyond your budget or expertise so here's a fresh solution to the perennial problem of making over that most costly of items – a truly comfortable sofa. It takes the conventional gambit, a throw, one step further by using a cotton dustsheet, which must be some of the cheapest fabric around, and it accepts the real disadvantage of throws – they just don't stay put. Using nappy pins, the odd button and (in the case of the chair I've thrown in for free) stout rubber bands, these covers will survive the heaviest video session.

MATERIALS

Dyeing ▶ 1 new cotton dustsheet (approx. 3.3 x 3.3m/3⅔ x 3⅔yd/ detergent / 200g yellow cold-wash hand dye / water according to the manufacturer's instructions / 500g salt Preparing the pins ▶ 54 nappy pins / 100ml yellow fast-drying enamel spray paint Covering the sofa ▶ 108 small green beads / 108 small red beads / 4 red buttons / red thread / 3 green buttons / green thread

EQUIPMENT

Washing machine / plastic dustsheet / rubber gloves / plastic dustbin or large container for dyeing / mixing stick / iron / masking tape / scissors / approx. 2.5cm (1in) polystyrene (30.5cm2/12in2) / protective mask / semi-circular upholstery repair needle or standard needle

METHOD
Dyeing

PROTECT YOUR WORK SPACE WITH DUSTSHEETS BEFORE SPRAYING, WORK IN A WELL-VENTILATED AREA AND WEAR A MASK.

1 Machine wash the cotton dustsheet five times, using your usual detergent, and hang to dry naturally. This sounds laborious, I know, but learn from my mistakes. First, it takes that many washes to remove all traces of the manufacturer's finish, which is essential if the dye is to take evenly. Second, tumble dry this fabric and it will shrink.

2 Protect your work space with the plastic dustsheet and your hands with rubber gloves. Following the manufacturer's instructions, make up the cold-water dye in a container large enough to take dye and dustsheet. I used a plastic dustbin, checked first for leaks and scrubbed thoroughly!

NO-SEW COVER FOR AN OLD SOFA

3 Again following the instructions, dye the dustsheet, rinse until the water is clear, wring out and hang to dry naturally.

4 Press, using a medium-hot iron.

Preparing the pins

1 Open each nappy pin, cover the metal sections with masking tape and stick into the polystyrene, spacing them as much as possible.

2 Shake the spray can well and apply two thin, even coats to the plastic parts of the pins with steady, sweeping strokes, allowing 1 hour for each coat to dry.

Covering the sofa

1 Lay the dustsheet over the sofa, draping it to conceal the original upholstery. Tuck in a little fabric at the back and sides of the seat where necessary and work out the natural folding places at each side, front and back. Arrange the fabric at the folds to form an inverted pleat.

2 Working from top to bottom and beginning just below seat level at the inner arm, use nappy pins to secure the pleat on each side at the front. Thread each pin with one green and one red bead, push the point through the folds of the pleat, and then thread another red bead and green bead before fastening.

3 Repeat the process to secure the pleat at each side at the back. These will be longer so, again starting from the top, use twenty pins for each side.

4 To secure the fabric on the arms, use the needle and thread to sew two evenly spaced buttons, one red and one green, halfway up each inside arm. Yes, I know I call it 'no-sew' but come on. You need to push the needle through the fabric and into the upholstery each time before drawing it out again – the special semi-circular repair needle I recommend makes the job very easy but it's not difficult with a standard needle. To remove the cover for washing is simplicity itself – just undo the pins and snip through the button threads.

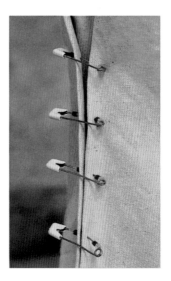

5 To secure the fabric at the front below the seat, sew on three evenly spaced buttons in the same way, a green button in the middle and a red one on either side.

NO-SEW COVER FOR A LOW CHAIR

COVERING A LOW CHAIR

MATERIALS

Dyeing the dustsheet ▶ ½ new cotton dustsheet (approx. 1.65 x 1.65m/ 1⅘ x 1⅘yd), plus half quantities listed for Sofa
Covering the chair ▶ 4 strong rubber bands / 12m (13ft) ribbon of three colours (dark green, blue and lavender) / 7 buttons / matching thread

EQUIPMENT

As Sofa, but omit masking tape, polystyrene and mask, and add sewing machine

METHOD

Dyeing

Follow the method described for the Sofa. Then turn and hand or machine sew the single raw edge – the other three are all selvedges – and press once more.

Covering the chair

1 Lay the dustsheet over the chair, concealing the upholstery and legs completely, and tuck in a little fabric at the back of the seat.

2 Working on the front of the seat first, use both hands to gather the excess cloth into two equal bunches, one at each side, and secure with rubber bands.

3 Form another two bunches at the back of the seat, one at either side, just above the point where seat and back meet. Check and adjust the drapery to your taste. The most practical and attractive effects are achieved by keeping the fullness at the sides so that front and back verticals are uncluttered.

4 Cut the three ribbons into varying lengths. Take one piece of each colour and twist round one of the front bunches, concealing the rubber band and leaving loose ends of different lengths. Repeat for the other front bunch. Vary the colours for the sides, tying some of the ends to form a bow.

5 To secure the fabric at the front, just below the seat, sew on three evenly spaced buttons, using the method described in Covering the sofa, step 4.

6 Secure the fabric at the sides in the same way. I used one at each side of the seat and another high on the sides of the back.

THREE WAYS WITH
A DINING CHAIR

It's easy enough to pick up cheap, sturdy, upright chairs in junk shops, though singletons are commoner than sets. That hardly matters if you pick a colour (or colours) and paint finish to unite them. In these three projects I've selected standard designs dating from the last thirty or forty years and given them a variety of simple treatments, traditional and contemporary, which could be applied to any number of other chairs. If my way with pop-up seats persuades you to reconsider the potential in some ponderous set of forties castouts with legs like barley-sugar twist, I'll be happy. Remember too: in small households where space and money is limited, one of the advantages of toning, multi-coloured sets of dining chairs is that they can be dual function – serving time in a bedroom or bathroom and only pressed into service when guests arrive. All that needs is careful colour co-ordination.

MACHINE-AGE METALLIC

CLEANING AND PRIMING

Remove pop-up seat and set aside for covering. Prepare the surface thoroughly by cleaning; prime with white acrylic spray primer. See pages 12–17; see also below for spray technique.

Opposite (left to right): Peach, purple and pale spearmint green top coats for a trio of sprayed chairs.

MATERIALS
for one chair (right)

Top coat ▶ 300ml peach metallic car spray paint
Sealant coats ▶ 300ml clear satin acrylic spray varnish (2 coats)
Re-covering seat ▶ 0.5 x 0.5m (18 x 18in) pale blue upholstery velvet

EQUIPMENT

Dustsheets / protective mask / hand-held staple gun and staples / scissors

METHOD
Top coat

PROTECT YOUR WORK SPACE WITH DUSTSHEETS BEFORE SPRAYING, WORK IN A WELL-VENTILATED AREA AND WEAR A MASK.

Shake the can well and spray with steady, sweeping strokes, holding the can 30.5cm (12in) from the prepared and primed surface. Aim for even coverage. Allow to dry (1 hour).

Sealant coats

Spray two even coats of varnish in the same way. Allow 1 hour for the first coat to dry, 2–3 hours for the second.

Re-covering the pop-up seat

1 If the seat fits only one way into its space, lay the square of velvet on top of it to decide which way you want the pile to lie. (Velvet has a light and a dark tone depending on how light strikes the pile.) This is important if you are covering several seats with one colour, unless you like the idea of using different tones.

2 Place the fabric right side down on a flat surface and centre the pop-out seat, topside down, on it.

3 Taking one edge at a time, fold the fabric over onto the underside of the seat and draw it taut. Staple to secure, making a line of staples approx. 2.5cm (1in) from the edge. Repeat on the remaining three edges. This step is much easier if you can enlist another pair of hands.

4 Use the scissors to trim away the excess fabric, taking care not to cut too close to the staples.

RUSH SEAT FROM ARLES

CLEANING AND PRIMING

Prepare the surface thoroughly by cleaning; prime only the wood. See pages 12–17.

Fabric paints on artists' duck canvas for a sunflower cushion: use a dabbing action and don't overload your brush. Iron to seal.

MATERIALS

Base coats (wood) ▶ 500ml premixed orange vinyl matt emulsion (2 coats)
Glaze coat (wood and rush) ▶ 250ml acrylic scumble glaze (transparent) / 100ml vermilion artists' acrylic colour / 3⅓tbsp cadmium red artists' acrylic colour
Sealant coat ▶ 250ml acrylic varnishing wax (clear)

EQUIPMENT

Mixing sticks / 2 x 50mm (2in) emulsion brushes / container for mixing glaze / lint-free cotton rags

METHOD
Colourwashing (wood)

See page 152, basic recipe, for the technique. Set approx. a quarter of the glaze aside to dye the rushes.

Dyeing the rushes

See page 172, steps 2–3, for the technique. I used the same brush as for the wood glaze, topside only.

Sealant coat

With a clean rag, apply a thin, even coat of wax to the entire chair, wood and rush, working it in the direction of the weave. Allow to set (1 hour) and then buff with another rag.

FIFTIES RETRO

CLEANING AND PRIMING

Remove the pop-up seat and set aside for re-covering. Prepare the surface thoroughly by cleaning. See pages 12–17. No priming is necessary under blackboard paint when working on wood.

MATERIALS

Base coats ▶ 500ml blackboard paint (2 coats)
Glaze coat ▶ 3tbsp acrylic scumble glaze (transparent) / 1tbsp mars black artists' acrylic colour / 1tbsp titian buff artists' acrylic colour
Sealant coat ▶ 250ml acrylic varnishing wax (clear)
Re-covering the seat ▶ 0.5 x 0.5m (18 x 18in) white matt vinyl for shower curtains and tables / 3tbsp black fast-drying enamel paint

EQUIPMENT

Mixing sticks / 1 x 50mm (2in) household brush / container for mixing glaze / 1 x 50mm (2in) emulsion brush / lint-free cotton rags / hand-held staple gun and appropriate staples / scissors / small, flat artists' brush

METHOD
Base coats

Stir the blackboard paint well and apply two coats to the prepared surface with the household brush, allowing 3–4 hours for each coat to dry.

Glaze coat

1 Pour the scumble glaze into the container, add the mars black and titian buff, and stir well.
2 Dipping just the tip of the emulsion brush into the glaze, lightly brush the surface in the direction of the grain. Allow to dry (1–2 hours).

Sealant coat

See Rush Seat.

Re-covering the pop-up seat

1 See opposite, steps 2–4.
2 Stir the black enamel paint well and, turning the seat topside up, use the flat artists' brush to decorate it with random, long, wavy lines. Allow to dry (1 hour) and replace.

A backpad can change a chair's profile as well as offering greater comfort. This one is secured with adhesive fabric fastenings and took the same amount of vinyl fabric as the seat. A fabric slipover minus padding would change the look too.

GIVERNY CHAIR

This is another of my favourite projects, yet it could hardly be simpler. The colourway, which owes more than a little to thoughts of Claude Monet's retreat at Giverny, cheers me up every time I look at it. The chair itself was stained black when I found it, and it must have started life as a sixties diner or kitchen chair, but it's now so scrumptious it would be a shame to hide most of it under some table top. Special pleading aside, what it usefully demonstrates is that some conventional surface like a chair can offer almost infinite opportunity to the imaginative. There's no rule that states chairs must be just one colour. I've seen successful pieces that take the notion much further than this. So go on, have fun!

Monet's water lilies also inspired the painted cushion. See the caption on page 100 for the basic method. Vary the size and shape of your brushes and don't wash them too often – it helps the colours merge.

CLEANING AND PRIMING	**Prepare the surface thoroughly by cleaning and priming as appropriate. See pages 12–17.**
MATERIALS	**Base coats (seat and shoulder rest) ▶ 175ml white vinyl matt emulsion / 3⅓tbsp turquoise artists' acrylic colour / 5tsp monestial green artists' acrylic colour (2 coats)** **Base coats (legs and rungs) ▶ 175ml white vinyl matt emulsion / 5tbsp permanent rose artists' acrylic colour (2 coats)** **Wax resist ▶ 100ml furniture wax** **Top coats (seat and shoulder rest) ▶ see Base coat for the legs and rungs (2 coats)** **Top coats (legs and rungs) ▶ see Base coat for the seat and shoulder rest (2 coats)** **Sealant coat ▶ 250ml acrylic varnishing wax (clear)**
EQUIPMENT	**2 containers for mixing paint / mixing sticks / 2 x 50mm (2in) emulsion brushes / 1 x 25mm (1in) round fitch / small, flat artists' brush / fine-grade sandpaper / lint-free cotton rags / water to dampen rags**
METHOD **Aged paint finish**	See page 144, Wax Resist, for the technique. On the seat and shoulder rest I used aqua under pink, reversing the colourway for the legs and the rungs of the back. I added the pink rings on the rungs with the artists' brush after distressing but they'd look better still done before; allow to dry (1–2 hours).
Sealant coat	Using clean rags folded into a pad, apply the varnishing wax, leave to set (15 minutes) and buff up with another clean rag.

TARTAN

If you thought tartan decoration was strictly for shortbread tins, think again. Find the right toning or contrasting colour combinations and you have a pattern to put a smile back on the saddest saleroom reject. The basic principles are explained on page 162, but don't be limited by the size of the rollers available. Some of the narrow stripes on these projects were hand painted, using strips of low-tack masking tape to protect the surrounding surfaces. Paint away from the tape to avoid 'bleeding' and remove gently before the paint begins to dry.

NOTE In all three projects: 'white' and 'premixed' refer to vinyl matt emulsions; all other colours are artists' acrylics.

Each was prepared and painted with white acrylic primer and protected with sealant (see pages 12–17 and 42–3).

Left: Here the verticals are set close. Colourway: base coat – 420ml white, 4tbsp dioxazine purple; 1st grid – 125ml white, 6½tbsp dioxazine purple, 2tbsp deep purple; grey horizontal stripe – 100ml white, 100ml middle grey; 2nd grid – 4tbsp white, 2tbsp oxide of chromium green.

Above: This strict pattern with a generous eye for colour needs room to flaunt its complexities. Note how I've wrapped it over the sides – much more dynamic than centring. Colourway: base coat – premixed deep terracotta; legs and 1st grid – premixed deep blue; 2nd grid – (green stripe) 2½tbsp white, 2½tbsp oxide of chromium green, (purple stripe) 100ml white, 3⅓tbsp dioxazine purple; 3rd grid (liners) – use remains of 2nd.

A budget-store
pine chest gets
sunny style.
Colourway: see
page 163.

DECORATED
LOOM CHAIRS

If you find a loom chair in a junk shop or are lucky enough to inherit one, check what it's made of before attacking it with a paint brush. The originals are much sought after and, sadly, once repainted they cannot be stripped because they were woven not of rattan but paper, wrapped around wire. However, loom chairs have become so popular in recent years that it is easy to find copies or updates of the styles first created in the twenties and thirties. My stencil designs have a soft period feel which suits them admirably and can be applied either with sprays or the traditional brush. Unless your loom has already been heavily painted, I recommend spray for the top coat.

PEAR MOTIF – USING SPRAYS

CLEANING AND PRIMING

Prepare the surface thoroughly by cleaning; prime with white acrylic spray primer. See pages 12–17; see also page 99 for spray technique.

MATERIALS

Top coat ▶ 800ml antique white acrylic spray paint
Stencilling ▶ 200ml mint green acrylic spray paint / 200ml moss green acrylic spray paint
Sealant coat ▶ 800ml satin acrylic spray varnish

EQUIPMENT

Dustsheets / protective mask / photocopier / approx. 40 x 40cm (16 x 16in) stencil card / masking tape / scalpel / cutting mat / newspaper for masking / lint-free cotton rags

METHOD
Top coat

PROTECT YOUR WORK SPACE WITH DUSTSHEETS BEFORE SPRAYING, WORK IN A WELL-VENTILATED AREA AND WEAR A MASK.
Using the same spray technique (see Priming), apply an even coat of antique white and allow to dry (1 hour).

DECORATED LOOM CHAIRS

Stencilling

See page 157, Spraying, for the technique of cutting and using a stencil, and page 183 for the motif. I applied it randomly all over the chair, using mint green for the pears and the darker, moss green for the leaves and carefully adding a little moss green on one side of the pears to create shading.

Sealant coat

Spray a good, even coat of varnish to the entire chair. Allow to dry (1–2 hours).

Page 106: The Rose Motif is a hybrid. The primer (see Pear Motif), the top coat (800ml pink acrylic spray paint) and the sealant were all sprayed, but the stencils were stippled. Stencil colourway: light pink – 100ml white vinyl matt emulsion, 3½tbsp permanent rose artists' acrylic colour; dark pink – 3½tbsp white vinyl matt emulsion, 2¾tbsp permanent rose artists' acrylic colour; green – 100ml emerald green artists' acrylic colour, 3½tbsp white vinyl matt emulsion; sealant – see Pear Motif. For motif, see page 183.

PEACH MOTIF – USING BRUSHES

CLEANING AND PRIMING

Prepare the surface thoroughly by cleaning; prime with white acrylic primer. See pages 12–17.

MATERIALS

Top coat ▶ 400ml white vinyl matt emulsion / 100ml cobalt blue artists' acrylic colour
Stencils ▶ 200ml white vinyl matt emulsion / 150ml cadmium orange artists' acrylic colour / 100ml pale olive green artists' acrylic colour
Sealant coat ▶ 800ml satin acrylic spray varnish

EQUIPMENT

See Pear Motif – omitting newspaper and substituting smaller stencil card (23 x 23cm/9 x 9in) – plus container for mixing paint / mixing sticks / 1 x 50mm (2in) emulsion brush / 3 saucers / 3 x 25mm (1in) round stencil brushes

METHOD
Top coat

1 Pour the white emulsion into the container, add the cobalt blue and mix well.

2 Apply evenly to the surface with the emulsion brush and allow to dry (1–2 hours).

Left: Peach Motif stencil colourway: light orange – 100ml white vinyl matt emulsion, 3½tbsp cadmium orange artists' acrylic colour; dark orange – 100ml cadmium orange artists' acrylic colour, 3½tbsp white vinyl matt emulsion; green – 100ml pale olive green artists' acrylic colour, 3½tbsp white vinyl matt emulsion.

Stencilling

See page 159, Stippling, for the technique, and page 183 for the motif. Here I used the paler peach tone over the whole fruit, then, with the second stencil brush, stippled one side with darker peach for shaping and shading. The third brush was used for the green leaves. See caption for colour mixes.

Sealant coat

See Pear Motif and follow the safety instructions. I decided to spray – it's so much easier to achieve a good finish on this surface.

THREE WAYS WITH
A METAL TRUNK

These three trunks were liberated from an aunt who'd discovered twelve of assorted sizes in an attic room when she moved into a new house several years ago. But once I'd spotted their potential, similar specimens seemed to turn up in every shop I explored. Dual function is the theme here – striking and attractive storage space plus some comfortable, but probably temporary seating. The scenario is yours to explore but I've come up with three very different looks which could find a place in a variety of spaces – from an elegant hallway to a teenage bedroom. Alternatively, adopt the seating idea but research naval or folk decoration for a period piece. Just one word of warning. Like the loom chairs, do consider your trunk carefully before you begin, and if it already has real character or period interest, take advice before trying to change or restore it.

VERDIGRIS ANCESTRAL

CLEANING AND PRIMING	**Prepare the surface thoroughly by cleaning; prime the inside of lid and entire outside with two coats of grey metal primer. See pages 12–17.**
MATERIALS	**Preparation ▶ 25 x 50mm (1 x 2in) battens / 19mm (¾in) MDF or plywood** **Construction ▶ 10 dome-headed brass screws** **Base coats ▶ 500ml blackboard paint (2 coats)** **Glaze coat ▶ 2tbsp acrylic scumble glaze (transparent) / 1tbsp monestial green artists' acrylic colour / 1tbsp titanium white artists' acrylic colour** **Sealant coat ▶ 500ml dead flat acrylic varnish**
EQUIPMENT	**For trunk – metal rule / pencil / adjustable work bench and/or G-clamps / tenon saw / medium-grade sandpaper / set square / ruler or straight edge / protective mask (if using MDF) / jig saw / drill with wood, 25mm (1in) flat wood and metal bits / screwdriver** **For paint effect – mixing sticks / 1 x 50mm (2in) household brush / container for mixing glaze / large plate / 1 x 15mm (½in) round hoghair brush / 1 x 50mm (2in) varnish brush**

THREE WAYS WITH A METAL TRUNK

Preparation

ALWAYS WEAR A MASK IF CUTTING MDF.

1 Measure the internal length and width of your trunk and make a note of those measurements – you will need to refer to them several times. Our trunk measured 50.5 x 73.5cm (20 x 29in).

2 To make the battens which support the board under the cushion, measure and mark two lengths and two widths on the 25 x 50mm (1 x 2in) timber, making both widths 5cm (2in) shorter than the internal measurement. This allows space for them to abut at the four corners. Our two widths were 45.5cm (18in) long.

3 Securing the timber with clamps, cut the four pieces as marked, using the tenon saw. Sand carefully to remove any rough edges.

4 For the board, draw a rectangle on the wood, using the set square and ruler (or straight edge). Make both length and width 2.5cm (1in) shorter than the internal measurements for easier removal. Ours was 48 x 71cm (19 x 28in). You could ask your supplier to precut to size if you prefer.

5 Clamp the wood, cut out the rectangle with the jig saw and sand any rough edges.

6 Use the flat wood bit to drill a hole approx. 7.5cm (3in) from each end of the board. You'll use these to lift it out of the trunk so make them large enough to take at least one finger comfortably. Again, sand the rough edges.

Construction

Ask someone to hold each of the battens in position as you drill holes for the screws which will secure them. The upper edge of the battens should be at the same height – approx. 2.5cm (1in) below the rim of the trunk, placed wide side down. Using the metal bit, drill from the outside to make three evenly spaced holes in the longer sides and two in the short sides. Insert the screws and tighten.

Verdigris finish

See page 167 for the technique. Again paint the inside of the lid and the entire outside. Stipple the surface details carefully for an authentically soft, patchy effect.

Sealant coat

Stir the varnish well and apply two coats to your painted surfaces. Allow 2–3 hours for each coat to dry.

MAKING THE CUSHION

Use flame-retardant foam for the filling. For the Verdigris and Gingham Trunks, I used a cushion 10cm (4in) deep, cut 12mm (½in) wider and longer than the board. For the smaller French Trunk, the cushion was 7.5cm (3in) deep. Remember that it must fit inside the lid when closed.

Cut two rectangles of tartan to fit, adding 15mm (⅝in) all round for turnings. I used approx. 2m x 140cm (6ft x 56in) of fabric for the two large trunks, 1m x 140cm (56in) for the small one. For the long sides, cut two pieces to fit, adding the 15mm (⅝in) allowance. Repeat for the short sides.

Machine sew the short ends of the sides together to make one strip. With right sides together and matching seams to corners, machine sew the long strip to one rectangle. Repeat to join the other rectangle, leaving one end open. Press the seams open, trimming and clipping the corners. Turn right sides out, insert the foam and oversew the open end.

COUNTRY FRENCH

CLEANING AND PRIMING

I chose not clean or prime this one so that the rust would break through quickly to enhance the aged effect.

MATERIALS

Preparation and Construction – see Verdigris Trunk.
This trunk was approx. half the size of the other two.
Base coat ▶ 250ml white vinyl matt emulsion
Top coat (outside) ▶ 250ml white vinyl matt emulsion
Top coat (inside) ▶ 190ml white vinyl matt emulsion /
4tbsp dioxazine purple artists' acrylic colour
Rust effect ▶ 3tbsp reddish gold acrylic paint

THREE WAYS WITH A METAL TRUNK

EQUIPMENT

For trunk – see Verdigris Trunk
For paint effect – mixing sticks / 2 x 50mm (2in) emulsion brushes / container for mixing paint / hammer / chisel / saucer / 1 x 25mm (1in) household brush

METHOD

For Preparation and Construction, see Verdigris Trunk.

Base coat

Stir the white emulsion well and, using one of the emulsion brushes, apply a good, even coat to the prepared and primed inside lid and entire outside. Allow to dry (2–3 hours).

Top coats

1 Stirring well, brush another 250ml white emulsion onto the outside only and allow to dry (2–3 hours).
2 Pour 190ml white emulsion into the container, add the dioxazine purple and stir well.
3 Apply to the inside lid, using the other emulsion brush. Allow to dry (2–3 hours).

Distressing the paint

Gently chip away at the edges and raised areas on the outside, using the hammer and chisel to reveal the bare metal beneath. Don't overdo it. Remember: the aim is to create natural ageing and battering, not some lost-property reject.

Rust effect

Pouring a little of the reddish gold paint at a time onto the saucer, dip just the tip of the small household brush and apply the paint carefully to the chipped areas. Here again, your aim is to suggest just the first stages of rust so don't cover the chips completely. Allow to dry (1 hour).

Making the cushion

See page 113. Contrasting piping would look great here.

BLUE GINGHAM

CLEANING AND PRIMING	**Prepare the surface thoroughly by cleaning; prime inside of lid and outside with two coats of grey metal primer. See pages 12–17.**
MATERIALS	**Preparation and Construction – see Verdigris Trunk** **Base coats ▶ 400ml white vinyl matt emulsion / 100ml cerulean blue artists' acrylic colour (2 coats)** **Rolling the grid ▶ 1st stripe – 160ml white vinyl matt emulsion, 6tbsp ultramarine blue artists' acrylic colour / 2nd stripe – 125ml white emulsion, 125ml ultramarine blue artists' acrylic colour** **External detail ▶ 2tbsp premixed deep yellow vinyl matt emulsion** **Sealant coat ▶ 500 clear dead flat acrylic varnish**
EQUIPMENT	**For trunk – see Verdigris Trunk** **For paint effect – 3 containers for mixing paint / mixing sticks / 1 x 50mm (2in) emulsion brush / Chinagraph or soft coloured pencil (to match stripes) / ruler or straight edge / set square / 2 large plates / 2 x 25mm (1in) foam seam rollers / 1 x 15mm (½in) flat artists' brush / 1 x 50mm (2in) varnish brush**
METHOD	For Preparation and Construction see Verdigris Trunk.
Roller tartan	See page 162. I rolled a grid of mid and deep blue stripes over two coats of turquoise. The external details were highlighted in yellow, using the artists' brush. Allow to dry (2 hours).
Sealant coat	See Verdigris Trunk.
Making the cushion	See page 113. Again, try piping – you can buy it ready made.

CRUSTACEAN

Forget those sad souvenirs. With colour and confidence you can use shells to create original focal points for bedrooms, living rooms and bathrooms. Gathered from the shore or bought from specialist stockists, the variety is extraordinary. Bed them in tile adhesive applied with a filler knife – don't be too lavish or it will be difficult to paint – and leave to dry (12 hours). Apply primer and top coat with a gentle, tapping wrist action for even coverage. Brush a little talc onto the top coat while still wet if you want an aged look; when dry, highlight detail with gilt cream. (See page 27 for adhesives, pages 42–3 for sealants.)

Left: Baroque splendour for a simple modern mirror. The new frame was cut from MDF or plywood (see template on page 183), glued to the old one and secured with panel pins. The main features – plaster cherubs, not shells – were bedded in first, followed by scraps of net curtain, arranged in folds stiffened with diluted PVA glue. Coins, beads and shells filled the empty spaces. Colourway: white acrylic primer; top coat – premixed mint green vinyl matt emulsion.

Left: This free-standing cornice, made with three pieces of 25 x 75mm (1 x 3in) timber, was glued and secured with panel pins. It looked best cut narrower than the cupboard. The beauty of the scallops and their position dictated a formal approach so small shells and beads fill the gaps. A silver-painted anagylpta border decorates each door frame. Colourway: white acrylic primer; top coat – see page 52, Top coat.

Left: Cooler colour and just a little talc play down the divine decadence, but the texturing is still exuberant. The fabric shade is sponged (see page 170, Glaze coat, using 125ml acrylic scumble, 1tbsp white emulsion, 1tsp dioxazine purple artists' acrylic), and decorated with flat shells and little pieces of seaweed from a bathroom potpourri. Colourway: white acrylic primer; top coat – as shade.

DECORATED
HEADBOARD

It was a friend's complaint that she just could not find a well-designed, wooden headboard for her trusty divan that set me thinking here. The answer was blindingly simple – mount bedroom cabinet doors on a supporting panel, add small side shelves for a light or midnight reading and decorate. But do note: this bed was only 1.37m (54in) wide. For a wider one, cut a larger panel on which to group or space your doors.

CLEANING AND PRIMING

Prepare the surface thoroughly before and after construction by cleaning; prime the front only. See pages 12–17.

MATERIALS

Preparation ▶ 12mm (½in) MDF or plywood (1 x 1m/39 x 39in)
Construction ▶ 9mm (⅜in) MDF or plywood, precut to size (48.25 x 155cm/19 x 61in) / 4 bedroom doors (38 x 45.75cm/ 15 x 18in) / 200ml quick-dry epozy glue / 12 screws
Base coat ▶ 460ml white vinyl matt emulsion / 2tbsp raw umber artists' acrylic colour
Mouldings ▶ 125ml gold leaf paint / 5tbsp cobalt blue artists' acrylic colour
Decoration ▶ 2⅔tbsp gold leaf paint / 3⅓tbsp vermilion artists' acrylic colour / 5tsp emerald green artists' acrylic colour
Ageing ▶ 150ml furniture wax (clear) / 2tbsp burnt umber artists' oil colour / 1tsp venetian red artists' oil colour
Fixing the headboard ▶ 25 x 50mm (1 x 2in) battens, cut to size (see below) / approx. 20 screws

EQUIPMENT

Photocopier / metal rule / scissors / pencil / adjustable work bench and/or G-clamps / protective mask (if using MDF) / jig saw / ruler or straight edge / set square / medium-grade sandpaper / lint-free cotton rags / water to dampen rags /1 x 50mm (2in) household brush / drill with wood bit / screwdriver / container for mixing paint / mixing sticks / 1 x 50mm (2in) emulsion brush / 2 small, flat artists' brushes / 3 artists' detail brushes / 5 saucers / A2 stencil card / masking tape / cutting mat / scalpel / 1 x 15mm (½in) stencil brush / tenon saw

METHOD
Preparation

ALWAYS WEAR A MASK IF CUTTING MDF.

1 Using a photocopier, enlarge the two shelf templates (for the base and backplate) on page 184 to size. The base sections of our shelves measured 16cm (6¼in) at their widest point, and our backplates were 14cm (5½in) high. Cut out.

2 Lay the templates for both sections on the 12mm (½in) wood and, using the pencil, draw round the shapes. You need to cut two copies of each piece.

3 Clamp the wood to secure and cut out with the jig saw.

DECORATED HEADBOARD

Construction

1 Use the ruler (or straight edge), set square and pencil to mark a line 12mm (½in) from the edge on all four sides of the precut sheet of wood. This defines the area where the doors are to be positioned – lay them down to check for fit.

2 Sand the backs of the doors and wipe clean with damp rag. Apply epozy glue to both surfaces with the household brush, and position the doors. Allow to dry (12 hours).

3 You need two pairs of hands to assemble the shelves. Clamp one of the backplates upside down and place a base section on top of it, at right angles and aligned with the tapering end of the backplate. Carefully drill two screw holes through the base and into the backplate and screw together. Repeat for the other shelf.

4 Clamp the headboard face down on your work surface so that at least 20cm (8in) overhangs the edge. Then clamp the shelves in their appropriate positions on either side with the overlapping sections of the backplates uppermost. Drill eight screw holes though each backplate into the headboard and screw together.

Base coat

1 Pour the emulsion into the container, add the raw umber and stir well.

2 Apply an even coat to the prepared and primed surface with the emulsion brush. Allow to dry (2–3 hours).

Mouldings

1 Stir the gold paint well and, using one of the flat artists' brushes, paint the outer moulding of each door frame and a narrow band around each front edge. Allow to dry (1 hour).

2 Using one of the detail brushes, paint the edges of the shelves with gold paint and allow to dry (1 hour). Our doors had a slightly raised central section which partly echoed the shape of the inner moulding of the door frame so I also applied a narrow band of gold paint approx. 6mm (¼in) wide at the edge of each of them too.

3 Place the cobalt blue in a saucer and stir well. Using the other flat brush, apply to the inner moulding of each door frame. Allow to dry (1 hour).

Decoration

I used a mixture of stencilling (for the initials and bee motifs) and freehand painting (for the flowers). The stencils were placed first, using gold paint: see page 159, Stippling, for making and using stencils, and page 184 for the bee motif. Books and magazines offer an enormous variety of references for type styles – photostat a few and experiment before making stencils for your chosen initials. (I'm not sure which came first, the initials or the bee, but both were clearly inspired by Napoleon and Josephine.) The flowers were added with two detail brushes, the vermilion before the green – both colours being placed on saucers and stirred well – and each colour was allowed to dry (30 minutes).

Ageing

1 Using medium-grade sandpaper, rub the surface in the direction of the grain to distress the decoration and reveal some of the base coat beneath. Wipe clean with damp rags.

2 See page 146, Ageing with Wax, to age further (and seal) with a dark wax.

Fitting the headboard

Detail will vary according to the style of your bed base, but the basic approach will be the same. Two 25 x 50cm (1 x 2in) battens are cut with the tenon saw and screwed to the back of the headboard and to the bed base or legs. Their length is determined by two things: the position of the lower fixing and the height you want the bedhead to be.

FABRIC BEDHEADS

Here's another advance in the crusade for imaginative bedheads. This time the emphasis is on fabric and the focus is single beds, although all three designs could be adapted for a double. Looking at the final results, what impresses me most is how easy it is to create a different look with the same basic idea – something it would be fun to explore with the quarter-tester – and how large a part the bedhead can play in setting the mood of a room, from the romantic to the practical.

MOORISH QUARTER-TESTER

CLEANING AND PRIMING

Prepare the surface after construction by cleaning and priming the outside of the tester and fronts of the tiebacks. See pages 12–17.

MATERIALS

Preparation ▶ 9mm (⅜in) MDF or plywood (1 x 1m/39 x 39in) / 25 x 50mm (1 x 2in) batten (0.5m/½yd) / 38mm (1½in) dowel (0.5m/½yd)
Construction ▶ 150ml PVA wood glue / 10 panel pins / 150ml fine-grade, ready-mixed wood filler / 2 glass curtain finials
Base coat ▶ 100ml silver spray paint
Glaze coat ▶ 150ml acrylic scumble glaze (transparent) / 2tbsp payne's grey artists' acrylic colour / 2tsp mars black artists' acrylic colour
Sealant coat ▶ 250ml clear matt acrylic varnish
Fitting the curtains ▶ cotton muslin (7m x 120cm/7½yd x 48in) / 1 reel matching thread / 250ml silver fabric paint
Mounting the bedhead ▶ 6 screws and wall fixings (see pages 27–8) / 0.5m (18in) steel wire / 30–40 metal beads / 6 small eyelets

EQUIPMENT

Photocopier / scissors / pencil / adjustable work bench and/or G-clamps / protective mask (if using MDF and for spray paint) / jig saw / medium-grade sandpaper / metal rule / drill with wood and masonry bits / tenon saw / 1 x 15mm (½in) round fitch / pin or tack hammer / filler knife / screwdriver / masking tape (optional) / plastic dustsheet / container for mixing glaze / mixing stick / large plate / 1 x 15mm (½in) round hoghair brush / 1 x 25mm (1in) varnish brush / iron / needle / sewing machine (optional) / clean dustsheet / small, round artists' brush / hand-held staple gun and appropriate staples / spirit level / ruler or straight edge / tin snips / pliers

METHOD
Preparation

ALWAYS WEAR A MASK IF CUTTING MDF OR SPRAYING. PROTECT YOUR WORK SPACE WITH DUSTSHEETS AND WORK IN A WELL-VENTILATED AREA.

1 Using a photocopier, enlarge the templates for the tester and the tiebacks on page 184 to the appropriate size. The front section of our tester was 35cm (13¾in) wide. You can make the tester bigger, of course, but you are likely to run into assembly problems if you make it smaller.

2 Cut out the full-sized templates, lay them on the wood and use a pencil line to make one copy of the front section, two of the side section, and two of the tieback backplate.

3 Secure the wood with G-clamps and carefully cut out all five shapes, using the jig saw. Rub with sandpaper to smooth any rough edges.

4 Measure, mark and then drill a central screw hole on in each tieback backplate.

5 Using the tenon saw, trim the batten to the width of the front section of the tester minus 18mm (¾in), which is the joint thickness of the two side sections. Drill a screw hole 5cm (2in) from either end of the batten through its 25mm (1in) section. These screw holes will be used when attaching the tester to the wall.

6 Cut two 12.5cm (5in) lengths of dowel, using the tenon saw. Drill a small pilot hole at each end of both.

Construction

1 To assemble the tester, use the fitch to brush a thin strip of PVA wood glue onto the back of either side of the front section and position the side pieces at right angles to it. Working from the front of the tester and using the pin hammer, tap four panel pins into each side to secure. Allow to dry (1 hour).

2 Glue the batten into the back of the tester at the base to form the fourth side of the rectangle and secure with a panel pin tapped in through either side.

3 Plug any holes with wood filler (applied with the filler knife), allow to dry (30 minutes) and sand off.

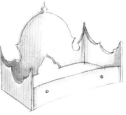

4 To assemble the tiebacks, attach the dowels to the backplates, screwing through the central holes from the back of the backplates, and then screw the finials into the free ends of the dowels. If you're worried about getting paint on the glass, mask them or attach them when mounting the bedhead.

Pewter finish   See page 166 for the technique.

Sealant coat   Brush on an even coat of varnish and allow to dry (4 hours).

Fitting the curtains

1 Press carefully with an iron before cutting the fabric in half to make two curtains – ours were both 3.5m (11½ft) long. Hem the sides and bottom of each one, using a machine for speed.

2 Protect your working surface with the dustsheet, stir the silver paint well and use the artists' brush to paint random swirls and dots on both curtains. Allow to dry (20 minutes).

3 To seal the paint, turn the fabric over and press the reverse with a medium iron.

4 Using the needle and cotton, gather the unhemmed top of one curtain to fit half the tester. Check for fit – you are aiming for even pleating from the inside front right round to the wall – and then staple into position, again working from the front. Repeat for the other curtain.

Mounting the bedhead

1 Another pair of hands is essential for this stage. Decide the height of the tester. Draw two faint pencil lines on the wall to mark the position of the batten at the back and check that they are straight, using the spirit level. Mark the positions of the two screw holes – they must correspond exactly to the holes you drilled in the batten.

2 Using the masonry bit, drill the holes and secure the tester as appropriate (see pages 27–8).

3 Drape one curtain as shown to help you decide the height and position of the tiebacks. Mark and then check the placing of each backplate on the wall with the spirit level and a ruler (or straight edge) before using the masonry bit to drill

through the top and bottom of each backplate into the wall.

4 Secure as appropriate (see pages 27–8) and drape the fabric.

5 Cut the wire into three pieces, using the tin snips, and twist a retaining loop at one end of each piece with the pliers. Thread the beads and hang each length on an eyelet screwed into the lower edge of the tester, making pilot holes with the bradawl.

FABRIC BEDHEADS

SHAKER HANGING

CLEANING AND PRIMING

Prepare the surface thoroughly by cleaning after preparation and priming just the front of the peg rail. See pages 12–17.

MATERIALS

Preparation ▸ Shaker or similar peg rail
Base and top coats ▸ 100ml white vinyl silk emulsion / 300ml red violet artists' acrylic colour / 3⅓tbsp deep violet artists' acrylic colour 3⅓tbsp permanent violet artists' acrylic colour
Sealant coat ▸ 150ml furniture wax (clear)
Preparing the hanging ▸ 2.5m x 140cm (8¼ft x 56in) natural, unbleached, curtain-weight linen / 1 reel matching thread
Stamping the motifs ▸ 1 x 100ml brown rubber-stamp fabric ink pad
Fixing the peg rail ▸ screws and wall fixings (see pages 27–8)

EQUIPMENT

Container for mixing paint / mixing stick / 1 x 25mm (1in) emulsion brush / lint-free cotton rags / metal rule / scissors / iron / sewing machine / 25mm (1in) wide ruler / needle / pins / assorted rubber stamps / spirit level / straight edge / drill with masonry bit, plus, if required (see Preparation), adjustable work bench and/or G-clamps tenon saw / wood bit / medium-grade sandpaper

METHOD
Preparation

If you need to shorten your peg rail, secure it with clamps, measure and cut to size, using the tenon saw. Ours was 157.5cm (62in) long. Sand any rough edges and remember to drill a new screw hole at the cut end.

Base and top coats

Pour the white emulsion into the container, add all three violets and stir well. Apply two coats to the prepared and primed surfaces, allowing 2–3 hours for each to dry.

Sealant coat

Using a clean rag and a circular movement, apply the wax to the painted surfaces and allow to set (15 minutes). Buff up with a clean rag.

Preparing the hanging

1 For the hanging, measure and cut one piece of fabric 1.17m (46in) deep x 2.06m (81in) wide. From the remaining fabric, cut 14 ties, each 35.5 x 10cm (14 x 4in).
2 To hem the hanging, turn 2.5cm (1in) under at the sides and bottom and 5cm (2in) at the top, press with an iron and machine sew.
3 Fold the ties in half lengthwise (right sides together) and press. Machine sew one end and the long side of each tie, leaving a seam allowance of approx 12mm (½in).

4 To turn the ties inside out, stand your ruler on end on a firm surface, place the short, sewn end of one of the ties over the other end, and roll the fabric down over the ruler, until the right sides have been turned out. Press, tuck in the unsewn ends and oversew.

5 Working on the reverse of the hanging, pin pairs of ties side by side along the top hem. Space the pairs evenly 24cm (9½in) apart, leaving approx. 10cm (4in) at either end. Machine sew to secure.

Stamping the motifs   See page 165, Using Ink Stamp Pads, for the technique. I used an assortment of ready-made leaf and feather designs.

Fixing the peg rail   Decide the position of the rail, mark and check with a spirit level and straight edge. Drill the holes in the wall, using the masonry bit, and secure as appropriate (see pages 27–8).

FABRIC BEDHEADS

NAUTICAL BANNER

CLEANING   Prepare the surface thoroughly. See pages 12–17. Do not prime.

MATERIALS   **Staining the pole ▶** 150ml acrylic varnishing wax (clear) / 3⅓tbsp emerald green artists' acrylic colour / 38mm (1½in) dowel, precut to size (157.5cm/62in long)
Preparing the banner ▶ 1.5m x 130cm (5ft x 51in) artists' 9oz duck canvas / 1 reel matching thread
Stencilling the flags ▶ 200ml fabric paint in white, yellow, ultramarine and bright red / black fabric pen with medium nib
Fixing the banner ▶ 2 large ring screw-in curtain finials / 2 brass brackets to fit dowel, plus screws and wall fixings (see pages 27–8)

EQUIPMENT   Container for mixing stain / mixing stick / 1 x 25mm (1in) household brush / metal rule / scissors / iron / sewing machine / set square / ruler or straight edge / pencil / photocopier / 2 x A2 stencil cards / masking tape / scalpel / cutting mat / lint-free cotton rags / 4 saucers / 4 x 25mm (1in) stencil brushes / pins / spirit level / drill with masonry bit

METHOD
Staining the pole

1 Pour the wax into the container, add the emerald green and stir well.
2 Using the household brush, apply the stain to the prepared surface in the direction of the grain. Take care not to overload the brush. Allow to dry (2–3 hours).

Preparing the banner

1 For the banner, measure and cut one piece of canvas 137cm (54in) deep x 150cm (59in) wide and four flag pockets, each 22cm (8½in) deep x 32.5cm (12¾in) wide.
2 Turn under 2.5cm (1in) at the sides of the banner and 5cm (2in) at bottom to make a hem. Take a 10cm (4in) turning at the top to create a casing or open-ended hem for the pole. Press with a hot iron and machine sew.
3 Turn under 2.5cm (1in) on all four sides of the pockets and press, again with a hot iron.
4 Use the metal rule, ruler (or straight edge), set square and pencil to mark the positions of all the flags on the front of the banner (the side without hems). The photograph on page 185 gives a complete view of it: the top row is approx. 10cm (4in) from the upper edge, the bottom row 16.5cm (6½in) from the lower edge, with a 5cm (2in) margin at both sides.

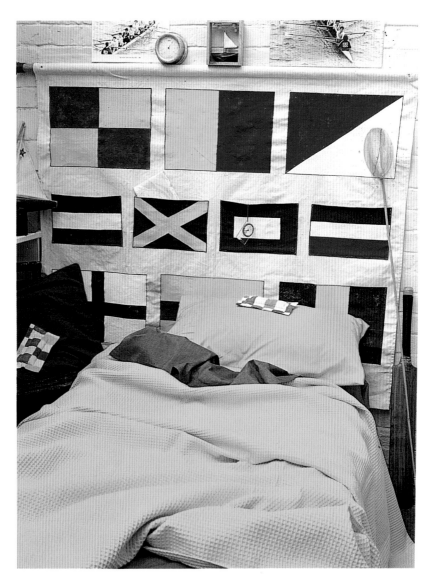

Stencilling the flags

See page 159, Stippling, for making and using stencils, and page 185 for the motifs and colour guide. I used ready-mixed fabric paints and drew lines around the completed flags with a fabric pen and ruler to neaten. Iron the reverse of the canvas carefully on a medium setting to seal the paint.

Finishing the banner

1 Pin the pockets in position as marked to form the centre row, keeping the pins away from the edges.

2 Machine sew approx. 6mm (¼in) from the edge around the sides and bottom of each one.

3 Push the pole through the casing at the top. Screw in the finials.

Fixing the banner

Decide the bracket positions, mark and check with a spirit level and straight edge. Drill the holes in the wall, using a masonry bit, and secure as appropriate (see pages 27–8).

DOUBLE BED
TO FOUR POSTER

The principle behind the transformation of this simple pine bedframe is extremely versatile. Change the fabric for something pale and floaty with a paint finish to match and you've exchanged drama for romance. And, on a more practical note, simple assembly means it's easy to transport if you move.

CLEANING AND PRIMING

Prepare the surface by cleaning before and after construction and by priming. See pages 12–17.

MATERIALS

Preparation ▸ 31mm (1¼in) dowel – 4 x 193cm (76in) for posts; 25mm (1in) dowel – 2 x 129.5cm (51in) for end poles; 19mm (¾in) dowel – 2 x 198cm (78in) for side poles; precut by supplier
Base coat (posts) ▸ 270ml white vinyl matt emulsion / 2tbsp raw umber artists' acrylic colour
First stripe ▸ 160ml white vinyl matt emulsion / 4tbsp dioxazine purple artists' acrylic colour / 2tbsp cadmium red artists' acrylic colour
Second stripe ▸ 160ml white vinyl matt emulsion / 6tbsp yellow ochre artists' acrylic colour
Ageing posts ▸ 105ml furniture wax (clear) / 5tsp burnt umber artists' oil colour / 5tsp yellow ochre artists' oil colour
Base coat (finials) ▸ screw-in wood finials / 5½tbsp white vinyl matt emulsion / 2tsp burnt umber artists' acrylic colour
Size coat ▸ 100ml italian water-based size
Gilding ▸ 10–12 loose sheets gold dutch metal leaf
Distressing ▸ 5tbsp methylated spirits
Sealant (finials) ▸ 100ml transparent polish
Ageing finials ▸ 1tbsp cadmium red artists' acrylic colour / ½tbsp middle grey artists' acrylic colour / ½tbsp white vinyl matt emulsion / 1½tbsp water
Woodwash (base and poles) ▸ 100ml white vinyl matt emulsion / 3⅓tbsp cadmium red artists' acrylic colour / 3⅓tbsp middle grey artists' acrylic colour / 150ml water
Construction ▸ 20 screws, as required (see below) / 15ml fine, ready-mixed wood filler
Hangings ▸ 6m x 140cm (19ft x 56in) venetian red cotton / 3m x 140cm (10ft x 56in) ochre cotton / matching thread / 6 assorted shells / 150ml acrylic gold spray paint

DOUBLE BED TO FOUR POSTER

EQUIPMENT

Metal rule / pencil / adjustable work bench and/or G-clamps / drill with wood and 25mm (1in) flat wood bits / 25mm (1in) masking tape (two rolls) / chisel or heavy-duty Stanley knife / 6 containers for mixing paint, glaze and wash / mixing sticks / 2 x 50mm (2in) emulsion brushes / 3 x 25mm (1in) emulsion brushes / flat artists' brush / medium-grade sandpaper / lint-free cotton rags / water to dampen rags / saucer / 1 x 25mm (1in) flat bristle brush / disposable gloves / 1 x 25mm (1in) round, soft-bristled brush / clean dusters / fine-grade wirewool / screwdriver / step ladder / filler knife / tailors' chalk / scissors / pins / sewing machine / needle / iron / hand-held staple gun and staples

METHOD
Preparation

1 To mark the holes into which the end poles will fit, use the metal rule and pencil to make a cross 2.5cm (1in) from one end of each post.

2 Secure each post with clamps and carefully drill a hole 12mm (½in) deep, using the 25mm (1in) flat wood bit and marking the depth on the drill bit with tape (see page 29).

3 To mark the holes into which the side poles will fit, lay all four posts on a flat surface with the tops side by side and the drill holes all facing upwards. Quarter turn each one to the right and mark a cross at right angles to the first hole approx. 7.5cm (3in) from the same end.

4 Clamping as before, carefully drill all four holes approx. 12mm (½in) deep.

5 To improve the fit of the posts when screwed to the bed you need to flattten a strip approx. 2.5cm (1in) wide at the bottom of each one. The lengths will be determined by the height of your bed base – our strips were 38cm (15in) long. Position your posts to measure the required length(s), making sure each strip aligns with the upper hole at the other end.

6 Clamping each post in turn, use the chisel (or heavy-duty Stanley knife) to make the required strips.

7 Position each post against the appropriate bedleg and drill three evenly spaced pilot holes for the screws which will secure it once painting is completed.

Base coat (posts)

1 Pour the white emulsion into one of the containers, add the raw umber and stir well.

2 Using one of the large emulsion brushes, apply an even coat to the prepared and primed surfaces. Allow to dry (2–3 hours). Reserve any remaining colour here and after the next two stages for final retouching (see Construction, step 7).

Adding the stripes
(posts)

1 Starting at the base, carefully wind the masking tape round each post in spirals 5cm (2in) apart.

2   Pour the white emulsion into a second container, add the dioxazine purple and cadmium red and stir well. Apply to the unmasked stripe on each post with a small emulsion brush. Allow to dry (2–3 hours) before gently removing the tape.

3   Mix the white emulsion and yellow ochre and use the artists' brush to paint an ochre stripe on the cream, leaving a narrow cream stripe on either side. Allow to dry (2–3 hours).

Ageing the posts

1 Using medium-grade sandpaper, rub the posts lightly to reveal some of the base coat and wipe clean with damp rag.

2 To seal and darken, see page 146, Ageing with Wax, step 1. Apply the wax with a clean rag, following the direction of the stripes. Leave to set (approx. 15 minutes) and buff with another clean rag.

Gilding (finials)

See page 168 for the technique. I mixed a terracotta base coat to create a mellow effect and, before sealing, distressed the gilding by rubbing very gently to reveal some of the base colour. Use fine-grade wirewool and methylated spirits, dabbed on with clean cotton rag.

Ageing the finials

1 Place the white emulsion in a container. Add the cadmium red, middle grey, and water (a little at a time), stirring well to mix.

2 Apply, using one of the small emulsion brushes.

3 Work quickly over the surface with clean rags folded into a pad, removing any excess glaze but leaving some in areas of detail. Allow to dry (1 hour).

Woodwashing (base and poles)

See page 140 for the technique. I used a single wash coat mixed to create a toning venetian red.

Construction

ASK SOMEONE TO HELP YOU THROUGHOUT THIS STAGE.

1 Position and secure each post, using the screw holes drilled before painting.

2 Working at one end of the bed, fit one of the end poles into the two upper holes in the posts.

3 To hold the pole in position, drill a hole through each post and into the pole. Screw to secure. Believe me – a step ladder is essential. For safety's sake and for accuracy, you must be at the correct height.

4 Repeat steps 2 and 3 to erect the pole at the other end.

5 Using the same method, erect both side poles, fitting them into the two lower holes in the posts.

6 Screw in the finials.

7 Conceal the screws with wood filler, leave to dry (1 hour), and sand gently. Paint with the appropriate colours.

Hangings

1 Lay the red cotton on a flat surface and, using tailors' chalk and the metal rule, mark and cut four long pieces. Our bed was approx. 188 x 137cm (74 x 54in) and I made the pieces each 3m x 42cm (9¾ft x 16½in), adding 15mm (⅝in) allowance all round for turnings. You will need to adjust these measurements if your bed is longer or shorter, wider or narrower. If you do, remember to allow enough fabric for an elegant drape over the bed.

2 Using the same method, cut two pieces of the same size from the ochre cotton.

3 Lay one of the pieces on a flat surface, fold neatly in half lengthwise, measure 20.5cm (8in) from one end along the cut edges and mark with chalk or a pin. Carefully turn back the upper half of the folded fabric from this mark to make a diagonal fold. Pinning first if you prefer, cut along the fold and then, using your first cut as a guide, cut across the lower half. Repeat for the point at the other end. Now shortcut the process by using this piece as a pattern to cut a point at each end of all the other pieces.

4 Pair two red pieces to make one panel, placing them right sides together. Pin along the edges and machine sew, leaving one side of one point open. Repeat, pairing the other two red pieces, then the two ochre pieces.

5 Turning the right sides out, tuck in the raw edges, oversew neatly with needle and thread and press each panel with a hot iron.

6 Use the machine to topsew all round each panel approx. 6mm (¼in) from the edge.

7 Sew found objects to the tip of each point with needle and thread. I chose shells, drilled a hole in each one, then sprayed them gold and allowed them to dry (15 minutes).

8 Using the step ladder, drape the panels over both end poles and secure with the staple gun.

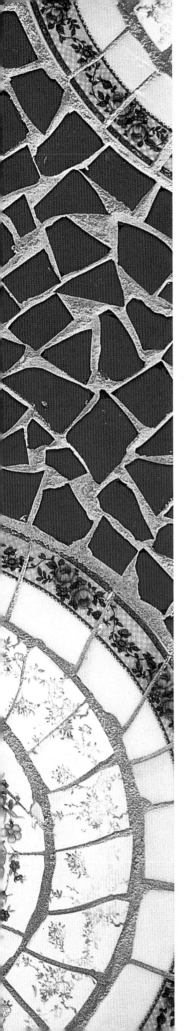

PART THREE

TECHNIQUES

A versatile range of paint finishes for furniture in traditional and contemporary colourways, plus decorative effects using ceramic, fabric, rush, glass and metal, all explained with step-by-step instructions

A wonderfully witty treatment for a mosaic table top: this effect was achieved with a mix of tiles and crockery. The tiles used for the blue background were probably broken randomly (see the basic technique on pages 174–6) but the 'plate' was certainly cut with tile nippers from several plates of varying size and carefully assembled.

ABOUT TECHNIQUES

This section of the book can also be used in two ways. On one level, it's a straightforward resource for the major projects and ideas spreads in Part Two. In that context it provides detailed instruction on how to achieve the various paint finishes and decorative effects cited there, frequently suggesting alternative colourways and illustrating additional small makeover projects, from shelves to deckchairs, from stools to firescreens. On a second level, like Part Two, this section can be the starting point for your own, totally original makeovers, providing endless scope for experimentation in a great range of different styles.

The paint finishes I've chosen to include are a hardworking bunch. Easy to apply and (with the notable exception of the dreaded but very simple lacquer) quick to do, they will all serve you well. Some, such as gilding, dragging, crackle glaze and colourwashing, have a long history – dragging, for example, was developed in the eighteenth century and used in the drawing rooms of the aspiring middle classes, who wanted the luxurious effect of fashionable silk-lined walls without the expense. Others, like woodwashing, have almost no past – I reckon it must have sprung from some universal need to redress the balance as the taste for pine-stripping reached saturation point in the mid eighties. But labels like 'traditional' and 'contemporary' are frequently meaningless where paint finishes are concerned.

An exercise in decoupage using aged music scores (see page 160) has created a subject which suits this classical room admirably. It's possible that the chest has less grand origins – the turned legs could have been added for gravitas. Note that the front itself is painted to highlight the basic structure.

Take dragging on page 150. My basic recipe for burnt umber on deep red does emulate the historical finish, using a darker on dark glaze, and works well on makeovers in period settings, whereas the light over dark effect in swatch 2 or the strong, 'modern' oranges of swatch 4 create a much more fashionable look.

Colour may be the defining element in any makeover scheme, but the technique is clearly important too. Take a good hard look at your 'raw material'. Can you achieve the look you want with it? If the

Left: This stocky cupboard is exactly the sort of piece likely to languish in a junk shop for ages waiting for someone to love it. There's no special technique to call attention to here. It's just a good example of the way you can make old furniture work for you. Gloss paints have been chosen for their tough, bright good looks, but in a child's room I would opt for water-based paints, sealed with silk acrylic varnish.

wood is not thick enough or the basic shape not suitable, change the game plan. Aged paint is never going to be a totally convincing disguise for the sleek lines of a wall of matt black laminate shelving.

But that said, some of my most successful makeovers have happened when I've ignored the cautious promptings of 'taste'. The metal effects on wood and laminate on pages 92–3 are a great example. Mix and match with some of the other decorative techniques I've included, using metal, glass, ceramic and fabric, and you have a wonderfully potent brew. Why not team punched tin with water-based crackle glaze or set decoupage on gilding?

Gain confidence and it's fun to experiment with mixing your own colours too. Using the basic recipes and the advice on pages 32–3 as your guide, it's a satisfying exercise to create a unique tone which exactly captures, say, the colour of a favourite fabric or a hand-painted tile picked up years ago on a foreign holiday.

Finally, some practical points to remember. If designing your own makeovers, do check the Preparation section on pages 12–17 and take account of the advice concerning sealants on pages 42–3. It's wise to practise your paint techniques on sample sheets primed with white paint first; hardboard or heavy card is adequate, though tests for woodwashing are best run on the appropriate wood.

Below: The wax-resist aged paint technique (see page 144) works best when used on sympathetic shapes. Try sienna tones for this colourway.

WOODWASHING

The name says it all – this simple technique creates a pale wash of colour on wood, leaving grain and any other surface detail still apparent. It's an almost instant upgrade for cheap, unpainted soft woods, new or old, although there may be some surface preparation before you begin (see pages 12–17). If you're prepared to strip, you can woodwash painted pieces too, but I don't recommend committing to the idea before you see what the wood is like. Only a limited range of commercial washes is available so making your own offers exciting scope for colour experiment. Single washes are fine but I illustrate the effects you can achieve with two – light on dark or dark on light.

BASIC RECIPE – ANTIQUE WHITE ON MOSS GREEN

MATERIALS

Quantities for Flexible Storage for Home Workers (see page 66)
First wash coat ▶ 210ml white vinyl matt emulsion /
4tbsp emerald green artists' acrylic colour / 1tbsp cadmium yellow artists' acrylic colour / 1tbsp pale olive green artists' acrylic colour / 175ml water
Second wash coat ▶ 270ml white vinyl matt emulsion / 2tbsp raw umber artists' acrylic colour / 175ml water

EQUIPMENT

2 containers for mixing washes / mixing sticks / 2 x 50mm (2in) emulsion brushes / lint-free cotton rags

METHOD
First wash coat

1 Pour the emulsion into one of the containers, add the acrylic colour and stir well.
2 Add the water (a little at a time) and stir again. You are aiming for the consistency of single cream.
3 Brush the thin wash onto the prepared but unpainted surface (see pages 12–17). Work wherever possible in the direction of the grain, which you will be able to see through the thin wash.
4 Using pads of clean rag, quickly wipe the surface to reveal more of the grain beneath. Allow to dry (1–2 hours).

Second wash coat

Mix and apply the second wash in the same way, using the other container and the second emulsion brush.

Notes If planning your own project, protect with a sealant for a hardwearing finish (see pages 42–3).

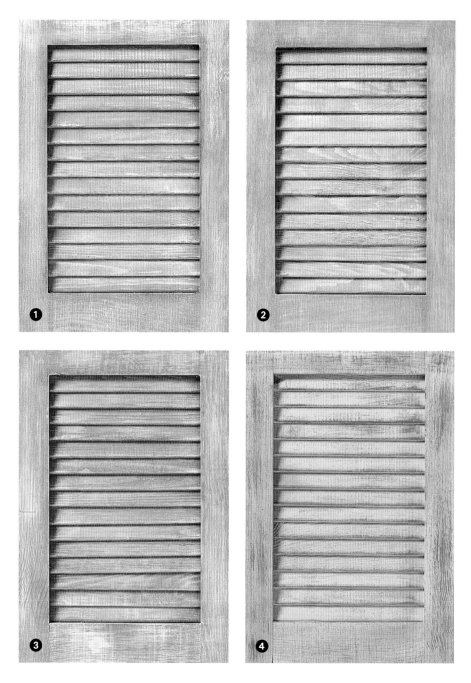

❶ ANTIQUE WHITE ON MOSS GREEN
The basic recipe: the use of a soft, creamy white over colour creates an appealing, almost sun-kissed look.

❷ RASPBERRY ON DAMSON
1st wash: 150ml white emulsion; artists' acrylics – 100ml dioxazine purple, 3½tbsp cadmium red. 2nd wash: 200ml white emulsion; artists' acrylic – 100ml rose pink.

❸ ANTIQUE WHITE ON RASPBERRY
1st wash: 210ml white emulsion; artists' acrylics – 3tbsp cadmium red, 1tbsp raw umber. 2nd wash: 270ml white emulsion; artists' acrylic – 2tbsp raw umber.

❹ MOSS GREEN ON YELLOW OCHRE
1st wash: 240ml white emulsion; artists' acrylics – 2tbsps cadmium yellow and bright green. 2nd wash: 210ml white emulsion; artists' acrylics – 4tbsp emerald green, 1tbsp each cadmium yellow and pale olive green.

HIGH-GLOSS LACQUER

Of course this is a cheat. The high-gloss finish of oriental lacquer, traditionally seen in black or red, was hard won by craftsmen prepared to lay down a thousand coats of resin, in later centuries paint, laboriously sanding each one back before the next was applied. Much as I love painting, I'm delighted that modern technologists with their tough, oil-based gloss paints can take most of the slog out of achieving this infinitely sleek, sophisticated look. Remember I said 'most'. This essentially simple technique still takes care and time but it is well worth persevering when the results are so stunning.

You need three other ingredients for success. The first is a good surface – no amount of subtle filling and patching will ever produce the mirror-like sheen that convinces. The second is a sound oil-based primer, which is why it's included here. The third is a dust-free place to paint. Good luck!

BASIC RECIPE – BRIGHT YELLOW

MATERIALS

Quantities for Contemporary Set of Drawers (see page 56)
Primer coat ▶ 500ml white oil-based primer
Lacquer coats ▶ 1½ litres premixed bright yellow high-gloss paint (5 coats)

EQUIPMENT

Mixing sticks / 2 x 50mm (2in) household brushes / wet and dry paper / lint-free cotton rags / warm, soapy water to dampen rags

METHOD
Primer coat

1 Stir the oil-based primer well and, using one of the household brushes, apply a good, even coat to the prepared surface (see pages 12–13, 16–17). Allow to dry (4–6 hours).
2 Rub the surface smooth with wet and dry paper.
3 Using clean rags and warm soapy water, wipe thoroughly to remove all the dust. Allow to dry completely.

Above left: The tough surface of a high-gloss finish is ideal for bathrooms, where condensation and changes of temperature can, in time, threaten some subtler effects.

Lacquer coats

1 Stir the gloss paint well. Apply an even coat to the surface with the other household brush, working in the direction of the grain wherever appropriate. Try not to drag the paint too much and yet avoid making short, fussy brush strokes. Allow to dry (12 hours if possible – 8 hours at least).
2 Rub down the surface with wet and dry paper, remove any dust with a damp rag and leave to dry.
3 Repeat steps 1 and 2 three times.
4 Repeat step 1 once more and leave to dry (12 hours).

❶ BRIGHT YELLOW
The lively colour used for the basic recipe has an essentially modern feel and works well in dark, sunless rooms. But swatch test it first – you may need to adjust your lighting.

❷ NEARLY BLACK
For industrial chic interiors, this dark grey with a hint of indigo will team successfully with chrome and steel.

❸ BRIGHT RED
A lighter shade of a traditional colour, red lacquer will sit alongside dark antique woods or austere minimalism.

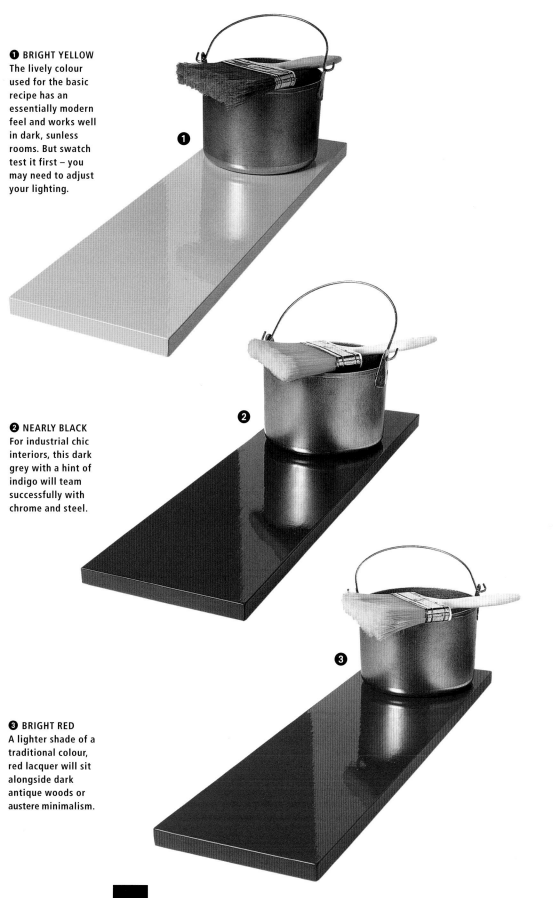

AGED PAINT

This group of techniques provides an invaluable aid for anyone keen to add a sense of history or character to undistinguished surfaces. All three are designed to simulate the effects of age on paintwork, either by distressing a painted surface to reveal an older, contrasting colour beneath or by mellowing or dulling down an original colour. You can, if you wish, take the process still further by literally attacking your surfaces with hammer and bradawl – the very opposite of that advice about preparing the surface before you begin.

BASIC RECIPE – WAX-RESIST METHOD

MATERIALS

Quantities for Bleached Wardrobe (see page 50)
Base coat ▶ 500ml white vinyl matt emulsion
Wax resist ▶ 150ml furniture wax
Top coats ▶ 375ml white vinyl matt emulsion / 300ml turquoise artists' acrylic colour / 105ml monestial green artists' acrylic colour (2 coats)

EQUIPMENT

Mixing sticks / 2 x 50mm (2in) emulsion brushes / 1 x 25mm (1in) round fitch / container to mix paint / fine-grade sandpaper / lint-free cotton rags / water to dampen rags

METHOD
Base coat

Stir well and apply to the prepared and primed surface (see pages 12–17) with one of the emulsion brushes. Allow to dry (2–3 hours).

Wax resist

Using the fitch, dab the wax lightly and evenly onto the areas where natural wear occurs – on knobs or handles, around the leading edge of doors and on raised panelling or details. These are the places where the base coat will be revealed when the top coat is rubbed back. The more wax you apply, the more worn will be the effect. Allow to set (15 minutes).

Top coats

1 Pour the emulsion into the container, add the colour and stir well.
2 Apply two coats to the surface, using the other emulsion brush. Allow 2–3 hours for each coat to dry.

Distressing the paint

1 Using sandpaper, rub back to the base paint at the areas where you applied wax. Be prepared to take time over this stage – you'll have to rub quite heavily.
2 Smooth any rough paint edges with a final sanding and wipe clean, using damp rags.

Notes If planning your own project, protect with a sealant for a hardwearing finish (see pages 42–3).

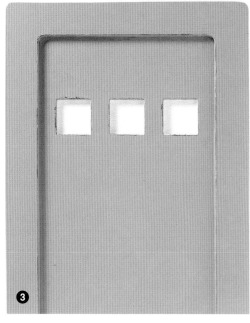

❶ AQUA ON WHITE
The basic recipe and most heavily distressed of the examples: note how sections of the frame and panel have been worked to suggest years of exposure to sun and sea spray.

❷ DEEP BLUE ON DEEP YELLOW
I used a little less wax and sanding for a colourway that reminds me of the Mediterranean. Both colours are premixed.

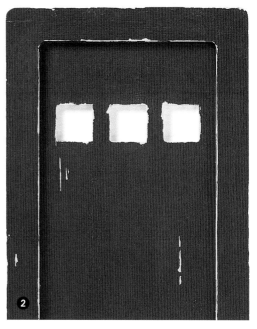

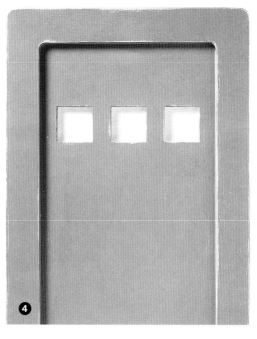

❸ LIME GREEN ON TERRACOTTA
Base coat: 290ml white emulsion; artists' acrylics – 150ml raw umber, 4tbsp chromium red. Top coat: 660ml white emulsion; artists' acrylics – 4tbsp emerald green, 1tbsp each cadmium yellow and pale olive green.

❹ LAVENDER ON WHITE
Treatment here and in example 3 is more refined. The result is a subtler effect, and one to try in rooms where you spend more time perhaps. Top coat: 690ml white emulsion; artists' acrylic – 4tbsp dioxazine purple.

AGED PAINT

BASIC RECIPE – AGEING WITH WAX

MATERIALS	**Quantities for Firescreens (see below)** **Wax coat ▶ 2tbsp furniture wax (clear) / 1tbsp yellow ochre artists' oil colour**
EQUIPMENT	**Saucer / mixing stick / lint-free cotton rags**
METHOD Wax coat	**1** Place the furniture wax on the saucer, add the oil colour and stir thoroughly. **2** Folding clean rags to make a pad, rub the wax evenly over the painted surface. Allow to set (15 minutes) and then buff up with another clean rag.

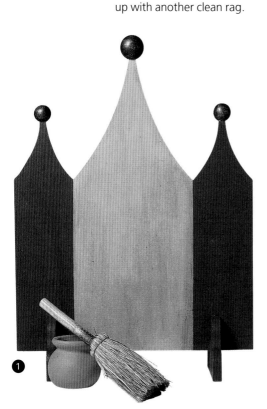

❶ WARM TONES
Some colours seem to warm as they age, and the way the creamy white base coat of the centre panel has taken the tone of the wax mixed for the basic recipe is a good example.

Base coats: (outer panels) 3⅓tbsp white emulsion, artists' acrylics – 2tbsp dioxazine purple, 4tsp cadmium red; (centre panel) 4tsp white emulsion, artists' acrylic – 2tbsp yellow ochre.

❷ DARK TONES
Most colours simply 'dirty' or darken naturally over time. This wax is tinted with a mix of ½tbsp payne's grey and ½tbsp mars black oil colour. Base coats: (outer panels) 2⅔tbsp white emulsion, artists' acrylics – 2⅔tbsp monestial blue, 4tsp payne's grey; (centre panel) 2⅔tbsp white emulsion, artists' acrylic – 2tsp raw umber.

BASIC RECIPE – AGEING WITH GLAZE

MATERIALS **Quantities for Shutters (see below)**
**Ageing glaze ▶ 5tbsp acrylic scumble glaze (transparent) /
1tbsp monestial green artists' acrylic colour / 2tsp payne's grey
artists' acrylic colour**

EQUIPMENT **Container for mixing glaze / mixing stick / 1 x 25–50mm
(1–2in) emulsion brush**

METHOD
Ageing glaze

1 Pour the scumble glaze into the container, add the colour and stir well.

2 Dip just the tip of the dry brush into the glaze and remove any excess on the lip of the container before applying evenly to the entire painted surface. Work in the same direction(s) as the previous coat of paint, glaze or varnish.

3 Using the same (empty) brush, work quickly over the surface again in the same direction(s) to distribute the glaze as evenly as possible. Allow to dry (2–3 hours).

Notes If planning your own project, protect with a sealant for a hardwearing finish (see pages 42–3).

❶ DARK GREEN The basic recipe is brushed over a mid green base coat of 3⅓tbsp white emulsion, tinted with 2tbsp monestial green and 4tsp middle grey artists' acylics.

❷ DARK RED Here I added 1tbsp cadmium red and 2tsp burnt umber artists' acrylics to the scumble glaze. For the base coat I used a premixed deep red emulsion.

WATER-BASED CRACKLE

This traditional form of paint distressing simulates the attractive crazing that appears on painted wooden surfaces subjected to temperature changes and will makeover even the ugliest plastic laminate. Originally undertaken only with oil-based materials, the results were always unpredictable. Fortunately, the water-based version is far easier to use. It is wise, however, to choose premixed emulsions and work on a warm, dry (but not hot) day. Colour choice is very important – use contrasting colours for a bold effect, closer tones for a softer, subtler look.

BASIC RECIPE – GREEN ON BLUE

MATERIALS

Quantities for Wardrobe Shelving (see page 60)
Base coat ▶ 750ml premixed bright blue vinyl matt emulsion
Crackle coat ▶ 600ml acrylic crackle varnish (transparent)
Top coat ▶ 750ml premixed bright green vinyl matt emulsion

EQUIPMENT

Mixing sticks / 2 x 50mm (2in) emulsion brushes / 1 x 25–50mm (1–2in) household brush

METHOD
Base coat

Stir the emulsion well and apply a good, even coat to the prepared and primed surface (see pages 12–17), using one of the emulsion brushes. Allow to dry (2–3 hours).

Crackle coat

Stir the crackle varnish well and apply one or two even coats with the household brush. The thickness of the varnish and the direction in which you brush will determine the size and type of cracks. To create relatively few, large cracks, apply two generous coats; one sparing coat will create much smaller cracks and so will one or two well-worked coats. For horizontal cracks, brush the varnish horizontally; for vertical cracks, brush vertically; for a mixture of the two, cross brush, applying one coat vertically and the other horizontally. Allow 1–2 hours for each coat to dry. The cracks appear as the varnish dries and begins to work against the base coat.

Top coat

Stir the emulsion well, brush an even coat onto the varnished surface with the other emulsion brush and allow to dry (2–3 hours). The cracks will begin to reappear within approx. 5 minutes as the contrasting or toning colour is thrown into relief. When the top coat is completely dry, the base coat beneath the varnish will be clearly apparent.

Notes If planning your own project, protect with a sealant for a hardwearing finish (see pages 42–3).

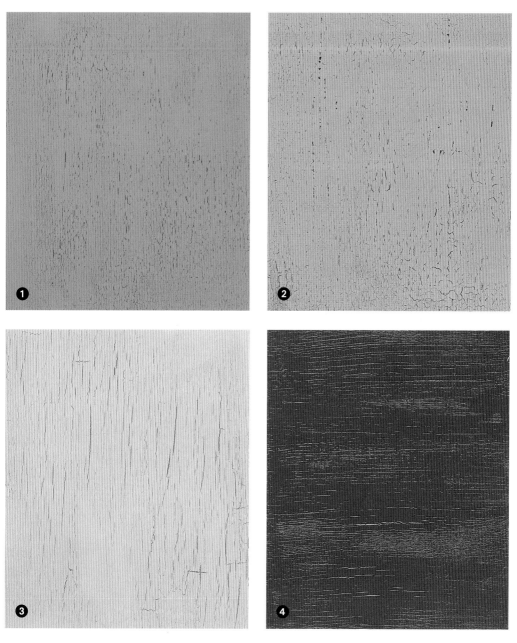

1 GREEN ON BLUE
The colourway used for the basic recipe, this swatch shows the effects of one sparing coat of vertical brushing.

2 LIME YELLOW ON PALE PURPLE
Vertical brushing again, but I applied two coats of varnish this time, working them both well. The results are similar, although the fine crazing is more evenly spread.

3 PALE PINK ON MOSS GREEN
Still more vertical brushing and again two coats of varnish, but now the crazing is negligible and the cracks are broader. Why? I was generous with the varnish but did not overwork it.

4 PALE PURPLE ON LIME YELLOW
The only example of horizontal brushing, here again I used two generous coats of varnish to produce broad cracks and just a little crazing.

WATER-BASED DRAGGING

Dragging derives from wood graining – using a long-haired brush, fine lines are drawn through translucent coloured glaze to reveal a base coat of a different colour – so it works well on furniture. This version of the traditional oil-based technique has much to recommend it. The use of standard emulsion brushes instead of specialist dragging brushes certainly cuts costs, as do the cheaper emulsions and/or artists' acrylics used to tint the glaze. Water-based glazes also dry more quickly than oil-based ones, and, although this could be a great disadvantage when working on large areas such as walls, it's unlikely to cause problems when painting furniture. In fact, scale works entirely in your favour. You are not going to face the problems of anyone trying to maintain a straight vertical line from ceiling to skirting!

Colour will determine the feel of the piece, and with natural tones on a neutral base coat you can even create the illusion of pale wood if the glaze appears to be applied in the direction of the 'grain'. I also like to combine dragging with decoupage for decorative or ageing effects.

BASIC RECIPE – BURNT UMBER ON DEEP RED

MATERIALS	**Quantities for Country Wardrobe (see page 54)** **Base coats ▶ 750ml premixed deep red vinyl matt emulsion (2 coats)** **Glaze coat ▶ 250ml acrylic scumble glaze (transparent) /** **3⅓tbsp burnt umber artists' acrylic colour**
EQUIPMENT	**Mixing sticks / 2 x 50mm (2in) emulsion brushes / container for mixing glaze / spare piece of board**
METHOD **Base coats**	Stir well and apply two coats to the prepared and primed surface (see pages 12–17) with one of the emulsion brushes, allowing 2–3 hours for each coat to dry.
Glaze coat	**1** Pour the scumble glaze into a container, add the colour and stir well. **2** Dip just the tip of the other (dry) emulsion brush into the glaze, remove any excess paint on the spare board and draw the brush downwards over the painted surface, using long, vertical strokes. You are aiming for a broken-colour effect so a little of the base coat should show through. Avoid pausing mid stroke if you can – it almost always shows – and, wherever possible, work in the direction of the natural grain of the piece. Allow to dry (2–3 hours).

Notes If planning your own project, protect with a sealant for a hardwearing finish (see pages 42–3).

❶ BURNT UMBER ON DEEP RED
The dark over light colourway of the basic recipe can work like an ageing glaze, suggesting the patina of time.

❷ WHITE ON CREAM
Base coat: 600ml white emulsion; artists' acrylics – 120ml raw umber, 2tbsp middle grey. Glaze colour: 3½tbsp white emulsion.

❸ DARK PURPLE ON PALE PURPLE
Base coat: 735ml white emulsion; artists' acrylic – 1½tbsp dioxazine purple. Glaze-coat colour: 3½tbsp dioxazine purple.

❹ DARK ORANGE ON LIGHT ORANGE
Base coat: 660ml white emulsion; artists' acrylic – 6tbsp cadmium orange. Glaze-coat colour: 3½tbsp cadmium orange.

COLOURWASHING

Colourwashing – the most familiar of the broken-colour techniques and the easiest – is normally associated with walls but it can be used just as successfully on furniture. The two methods demonstrated give lovely yet differing finishes and will look good in traditional and modern interiors. Once worked only in dark, sombre tones, colourwashing is now used with a vast array of colours to great effect.

BASIC RECIPE – DEEP RED ON ORANGE

MATERIALS

Quantities for Rush Chair (see page 100)
Base coats ▸ 500ml premixed orange vinyl matt emulsion (2 coats)
Glaze coat ▸ 250ml acrylic scumble glaze (transparent) /
100ml vermilion artists' acrylic colour / 3⅓tbsp cadmium red artists' acrylic colour

EQUIPMENT

Mixing sticks / 2 x 50mm (2in) emulsion brushes / container for mixing glaze

METHOD
Base coats

Stir well and apply two good, even coats to the prepared and primed surface (see pages 12–17), using one of the emulsion brushes. Allow 2–3 hours for each coat to dry.

❶ DEEP RED ON ORANGE
The basic recipe's hot, modern colourway needs careful placing.

❷ DEEP GREEN ON AQUA BLUE
Base coat: 440ml white emulsion; artists' acrylics – 2tbsps cerulean blue and monestial green. Glaze-coat colour: artists' acrylics – 5tbsps monestial green and cobalt blue.

❸ DARK BLUE ON SOFT GREY
Base coat: 440ml white emulsion; artists' acrylic – 4tbsp middle grey. Glaze-coat colour: 100ml prussian blue, 3⅓tbsp burnt umber.

❹ PALE BLUE ON BLUSH WHITE
Base coat: 440ml white emulsion; artists' acrylics – 3tbsp permanent rose, 1tbsp yellow ochre. Glaze-coat colour: 100ml cobalt blue, 3⅓tbsp white emulsion.

Glaze coat

1 Pour the scumble glaze into the container, add the colours and stir well.

2 Dip just the tip – approx. 2.5cm (1in) – of the other (dry) emulsion brush into the glaze and take off any excess paint on the lip of the container.

3 Apply with random strokes over the entire surface. Like dragging (see page 150), another broken-colour effect, you should still be able to see some of the base coat beneath. Highlight areas of detail with slightly increased coverage.

4 Using the same (empty) brush, go quickly over the entire surface again with random brush strokes – your aim now is to add more texture to the surface so the brush strokes remain apparent. Allow to dry (2–3 hours).

Notes If you are planning your own project, protect with a sealant for a hardwearing finish (see pages 42–3).

VARIATION – BRUSHING ON AND OFF

This is essentially another method of colourwashing rather than a different technique. You apply the glaze with a full brush, aiming for complete, even coverage, and then quickly rework the glaze surface with the same (empty) brush, using random strokes to take off some of the glaze and reveal the base coat beneath.

The final effect is softer and subtler than that of basic colourwashing. You see fewer brush strokes so the paint looks less fussed over or 'worked'. But, as it is more difficult to maintain a consistent texture for large areas, it's probably safer to use the basic recipe for, say, a wardrobe. Brushing on and off will also need protection for a hardwearing finish (see pages 42–3).

❶ PALE YELLOW ON DEEP PINK
Base coat: 375ml white emulsion; artists' acrylic – 125ml permanent rose. Glaze-coat colour: 5tbsp cadmium yellow.

❷ PURPLE ON LAVENDER
Base coat: 375ml white emulsion; artists' acrylic – 125ml dioxazine purple. Glaze-coat colour: 4tbsp dioxazine purple.

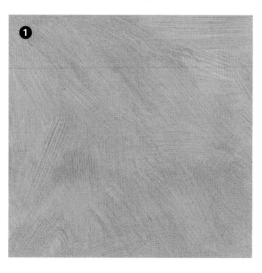

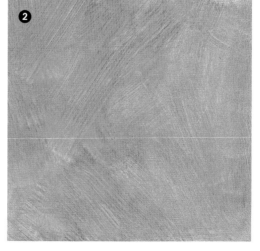

SPATTER ON A TEXTURED BASE

This technique sprang from experiments to create a stone effect with real depth for the Lapis Café Table and it really combines two in one – sponging (with some stippling on the side), plus spatter. I followed through with the sandstone stool and reckon, with a few colour trials, you could turn up a convincing granite too. But the third stool opposite took another, more imaginative direction – the combination of bright modern colours on a contrasting ground. All these colourways will probably look best on simple furniture with plain lines, and their busy, textured look might usefully conceal a less than perfect surface.

To return to my two-in-one theme, if you cut the spatter coats of the basic recipe entirely, you have an attractive, restful effect that could bring new life to depressing old bedroom furniture. Experiment with soft, toning pastel colours.

BASIC RECIPE – LAPIS LAZULI

MATERIALS

Quantities for Stool (see opposite)
Base coat ▶ 5tbsp white vinyl matt emulsion / 3⅓tbsp cobalt blue artists' acrylic colour
First glaze coat ▶ 3⅓tbsp acrylic scumble glaze (transparent) / 2½tsp ultramarine artists' acrylic colour / 1tbsp water
Second and third glaze coats ▶ 100ml acrylic scumble glaze (transparent) / 5tsp ultramarine artists' acrylic colour / 1tsp mars black artists' acrylic colour / 2tbsp water
First spatter coat ▶ 1tsp yellow ochre artists' acrylic colour / ½tsp water
Second spatter coat ▶ 1tsp titanium white artists' acrylic colour / ½tsp water
Third spatter coat ▶ 1tsp premixed acrylic gold paint

EQUIPMENT

Container for mixing paint / mixing sticks / 1 x 50mm (2in) emulsion brush / 6 saucers / assorted sea sponges / water for dampening and rinsing sponges / disposable gloves / 2 x 15mm (½in) round stippling or stencil brushes / dustsheets / 3 old, stiff-bristled round fitches / large piece of card for testing

METHOD
Base coat

1 Pour the emulsion into the container, add the colour and stir well.
2 Apply evenly to the prepared, primed surface (see pages 12–17), using the emulsion brush. Allow to dry (2–3 hours).

First glaze coat

1 Pour the scumble glaze onto one of the saucers, add the colour and stir well.
2 Add the water (a little at a time) and stir again. You are aiming for the consistency of single cream.

❶ LAPIS LAZULI
The basic recipe: this stone effect can be remarkably convincing given the right context. Small is best for lapis. I sealed all three stools with matt polyurethane varnish (250ml for 2 coats).

❷ SANDSTONE
Base coat: 5tbsp white emulsion; artists' acrylic – 3⅓tbsp cadmium orange. Two identical glaze coats total 150ml scumble glaze, 2⅔tbsp raw sienna and 3⅓tbsp water. Spatter-coat colours: 1st coat – 1½tsp payne's grey; 2nd coat – 1½tsp prussian blue.

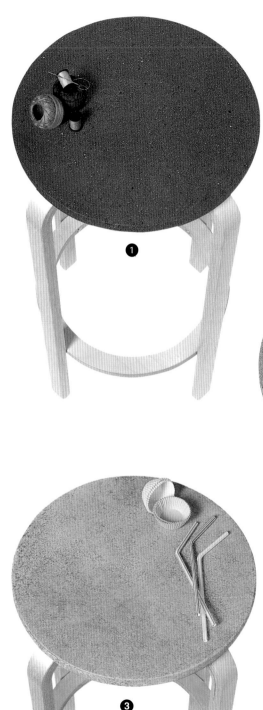

❸ YELLOW AND RED ON LIME
Base coat: 5tbsp white emulsion; artists' acrylic – 3⅓tbsp emerald green. Again, there are two identical glaze coats, with a total of 5tbsp scumble glaze, 2⅔tbsp emerald green and 3⅓tbsp water. Spatter-coat colours: 1st coat – 1½tsp yellow ochre; 2nd coat – 1½tsp vermilion.

SPATTER ON A TEXTURED BASE

3 Immerse one of the sea sponges in water and wring out until only slightly damp. Put on the disposable gloves and apply the glaze to the entire surface, using gentle, dabbing movements. Reload as required and vary your sponge from time to time to create interesting textures. Rinse them in water frequently so they don't clog. It's easy to overdo this stage – remember your aim is to leave some of the previous coat showing through. Keep the action light and avoid overloading your sponges. Allow to dry (2 hours).

Second and third glaze coats

1 Pour the scumble glaze onto a second saucer, add the colour and stir well.

2 Add the water, stirring again, and set half the resulting glaze aside on another saucer for the third coat.

3 Sponge on the second glaze coat, using the same method.

4 With one of the stippling (or stencil) brushes and a gentle, tapping wrist action, quickly soften the sponge marks. Allow to dry (2 hours).

5 Using the remaining glaze and the other stippling brush, repeat steps 3 and 4. By now you will have created plenty of texture and a translucency which will give the stone effect great depth.

First spatter coat

1 Place the first spatter colour on a fourth saucer and stir in the water (a little at a time). Again, you need the consistency of single cream.

2 Protect the work space with dustsheets before you begin. Wearing the disposable gloves, load one of the fitches with glaze and stand between 13 and 30cm (5–12in) from the surface. Hold the brush in one hand and use the fingers of the other hand to pull back the fitch's bristles, releasing a mist of glaze onto the surface. You are aiming for a series of well-spaced dots of varying size. Confidence is essential so try the technique out on a large piece of card first – you'll find that the further you stand from the surface the larger the dots are.

Second and third spatter coats

Using the same method, repeat to apply the second and third spatter colours.

Notes If planning your own project, protect with a sealant for a hardwearing finish (see pages 42–3).

I know stencilling is such a familiar decorator's tool it is beginning to be derided, but simple motfis used with restraint are an appealing, straightforward way to decorate plain furniture. Applied to painted or sprayed surfaces, stencilling can, for example, turn a hideous kitchen cabinet into an object of desire – or at least into something you can bear to look at until your budget allows for bigger changes! A flat surface is all you need. Use flat colour backgrounds, as I do here, or experiment with colourwashing (see page 152), sponging (see page 154) or woodwashing on previously unpainted wood (see page 140).

You can opt for speed with spray paint or go the traditional route with stencil or stippling brush. Naturally the results differ – spray can create even, uniform coverage, stippling will always produced a more textured look, and it takes some practice to achieve subtle shading with a spray can. Substitute fabric paints for artists' acrylics and you can stipple on fabric too – an idea for deckchairs, perhaps? (See page 170.)

BASIC RECIPE – SPRAYING A TWO-TONE DAISY

MATERIALS

Quantity for 3.5 x 3.5m (11½ x 11½ft)
Using the stencils ▶ 150ml rose pink acrylic spray paint / 150ml burgundy acrylic spray paint

EQUIPMENT

Photocopier / stencil card to required size / masking tape / cutting mat / scalpel / newspaper for masking / lint-free cotton rags / dustsheets / protective mask

❶ PINK AND BURGUNDY ON CREAM
The basic recipe: the strong colour contrasts and dense coverage create a bold motif of great simplicity. Base coat: 400ml pale yellow acrylic spray.

❷ TWO PINKS ON PRUSSIAN GREEN
The softer look of the petals is a matter of technique as well as colour. I used less spray and aimed for blush pink highlights with less even coverage.

STENCILLING

PROTECT YOUR WORK SPACE WITH DUSTSHEETS BEFORE SPRAYING, WORK IN A WELL-VENTILATED AREA AND WEAR A MASK.

1 Enlarge the two motifs – the daisy and the separate centre (see page 186) – to the required size at the same scale, using the photocopier.

2 Centre the photocopy of the daisy motif on a sheet of stencil card of the appropriate size, allowing approx. 10cm (4in) all round the image. Secure firmly with masking tape on all four sides. (If you plan to use your stencil for a repeating pattern, cut a square or rectangular piece of card. It's so much easier to line up and space the motifs.)

3 Using the scalpel and cutting mat, cut out the motif, neatly following the outline of the petals and the central circle. Press firmly through the photocopy and the card, aiming for a few 'clean' strokes. Lots of anxious little cuts make for uneven edges. Retain two of the three pieces – the daisy stencil and the circle cut from the centre of the motif.

4 Use the separate photocopied centre motif to make the smaller circle stencil in the same way. Throw the cut-out centre away to avoid confusion.

5 Attach sheets of newspaper to the sides of both stencils with the masking tape to protect the surrounding painted areas when you spray.

Using the stencils

1 Secure the daisy stencil to the prepared, primed (see pages 12–17) and painted surface, using tabs of masking tape and remembering to take some of the tack off first on clean rag.

2 Position the circular piece of card cut from the daisy motif so that it masks the middle of the flower.

3 Shake the pale spray can well and carefully apply an even coat into the unmasked area. Use steady, sweeping strokes and hold the can approx. 30.5 cm (12in) from the surface. Do practise on a spare piece of board first. It takes some experience to achieve even coverage. Remove both masks gently and immediately or they may bond with the surface. Allow to dry (1 hour).

4 Shake the darker spray can well and, placing the smaller circle stencil so that it masks all but the centre of the flower, spray carefully for an even coat. Remove immediately and allow to dry (1 hour).

Notes Positioning the daisy centre is easily done by eye, but you need to use register marks where fit is more critical. When working with the Vase stencils (page 58), for example, I matched light pencil marks on the vase shape with key points on the 'stripes' stencil (see page 39).

BASIC RECIPE – STIPPLING A TWO-TONE STAR

MATERIALS

Quantity for 3.5 x 3.5m (11½ x 11½ft)
Using the stencil ▶ 200ml premixed deep yellow vinyl matt
emulsion / 1tbsp titanium white artists' acrylic colour

EQUIPMENT

Photocopier / stencil card to required size / masking tape / cutting
mat / scalpel / lint-free cotton rags / container for mixing paint /
mixing sticks / 2 saucers / 1 x 15mm (½in) stencil brush

METHOD
Cutting the stencil

Follow the method described in Spraying, steps 1–3, to cut
the single stencil.

Using the stencil

1 See Spraying, Using the stencils, step 1.

2 For the pale colour, mix 150ml deep yellow emulsion with
the titanium white, stirring well.

3 Pouring a little at a time onto one of the saucers, dip the
stencil brush into the paint and dab it gently onto the entire
unmasked area with a light stippling or tapping wrist action.
You should be able to see some of the top coat beneath.

4 Stir the remaining (50ml) deep yellow emulsion well and,
using the same method and brush, apply the darker colour
down one side of the motif to sharpen the image.

5 Again using the same (this time empty) brush and action,
go quickly over the same areas to soften the meeting of the
dark and light tones. Allow to dry (1 hour).

Notes If planning your own project, protect all stencils with
a sealant for a hardwearing finish (see pages 42–3).

❶ TWO YELLOWS ON DEEP BLUE
The two-tone stars of the basic recipe are set on a hand-painted base of 500ml deep blue emulsion. The more textured effect of stippling is very apparent. Don't make the stars too small – the card 'bridges' will be vulnerable.

❷ TWO PINKS ON PALE GREY
Base coat: 410ml white emulsion; artists' acrylic – 6tbsp dioxazine purple. Pale pink: 6tbsp white emulsion; artists' acrylic – 2tbsps dioxazine purple and raw umber. Dark pink: artists' acrylic – 2tbsp raw umber, 1tsp cadmium red.

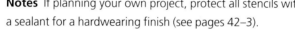

DECOUPAGE

Decorating a surface with shapes or illustrations torn from paper is a simple makeover technique. In our projects I've placed small tinted sections formally or randomly, combining them with paint finishes, but you can achieve striking results with total coverage. I've seen chunky shelves papered with typography and there's a gorgeous set of drawers decked with music scores on page 138. See Bibliography for sources.

BASIC RECIPE – AGED PAPER ON ANTIQUE WHITE

MATERIALS

Quantity for 3.5 x 3.5m (11½ x 11½ft)
Base coat ▶ 220ml white vinyl matt emulsion / 30ml raw umber artists' acrylic colour
Preparing the pieces ▶ photocopies as required / 2 teabags / 2tbsp instant coffee / 300ml hot water
Placing the pieces ▶ 50ml PVA adhesive or white glue
Sealant coats (interior use – see also opposite) ▶ 500ml clear, quick-drying, silk polyurethane varnish (2 coats)

EQUIPMENT

Container for mixing paint / mixing stick / 1 x 50mm (2in) emulsion brush / water to dampen paper and rags / small artists' brush / 2 cups / newspaper to protect work surface / saucer / 1 x 25mm (1in) household brush / lint-free cotton rags / varnish brush

METHOD
Base coat

1 Pour the white emulsion into the container, add the raw umber and stir well.
2 Apply two coats to the prepared and primed surface (see pages 12–17), allowing 2–3 hours for each coat to dry.

Preparing the pieces

1 Using water and the artists' brush, paint a line around each photocopied image to soften the paper fibres. Leave for a minute and then tear along the lines. Allow to dry. You are aiming for irregular, soft edges.
2 Lay the photocopies on the surface and decide their positions.
3 Put the teabags in one cup, coffee in the other. Pour 150ml hot water into each cup. Do not stir. Leave to cool.
4 Pour away the tea and wipe the teabags over the photocopies. Allow to dry (1 hour). Keep the teabags.

Placing the pieces

1 Protecting the work surface with newspaper, pour a little PVA glue onto the saucer and, using the household brush, apply a thin coat to the back of each photocopy.

❶ **AGED PAPER ON ANTIQUE WHITE** This is an extreme example of ageing with tea and coffee – it's your choice how far you take it.

2 Smooth each piece carefully into place with clean rag, making sure the paper lies flat with no bubbles underneath it. Allow to dry (2 hours).

Further ageing

1 Dampening the teabags if necessary, wipe over the entire surface, including the paint.

2 Pour most of the coffee away to leave just the granules and approx. 1 teaspoon of liquid. Dipping the tips of your fingers into the remaining coffee, flick a few granules over the surface (see page 39). Allow to dry (8 hours).

Sealant coats

For interior use, stir the polyurethane varnish well and apply two coats, allowing 3–4 hours for each coat to dry. For exterior use, substitute yacht varnish and apply three to four coats, according to the manufacturer's instructions.

TINTING WITH WATER-BASED INKS

❶ AGED PAPER USING SEPIA INK
Base coats: 500ml blackboard paint (2 coats). Tinting: 150ml sepia ink. Glaze: 150ml acrylic scumble glaze mixed with 100ml white emulsion and dry brushed. Sealant: see opposite.

❷ YELLOW OCHRE ON SHAKER GREEN
Base coat: 100ml white emulsion; artists' acrylics – 120ml hooker's green, 2tbsp yellow ochre. Glaze: scumble as above, tinted with 100ml yellow ochre artists' acrylic. Sealant: see opposite.

❸ ORANGE ON DEEP BLUE
Base coat: 250ml blue emulsion. Glaze: scumble as above, tinted with 3½tbsp cadmium orange artists' acrylic. Sealant: see opposite.

You can create a variety of effects by substituting water-based inks for tea and coffee. Place a little ink in a saucer, using the ink dropper provided. Dilute with water (1 part ink to 20 parts water) and apply to the photocopies with a damp cotton bud. Lightly dab with a dry, clean sea sponge to take up excess ink and eliminate brush strokes. Your aim is to seal and colour (not soak) the pieces. Allow to dry (1 hour). Place as opposite and then dry brush a glaze coat (see captions) and seal.

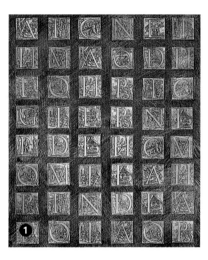

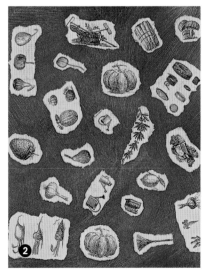

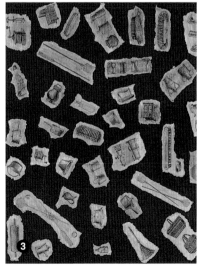

ROLLER PATTERNS

Gingham and tartan effects are easily achieved using seam rollers and are a lively way to customize flat surfaces. Colour determines the look and there's a wide range of patterns to copy or inspire. I've used artists' lining brushes to paint in narrow grids, varied the grid size and, on the CD rack on page 104, offset them for additional interest. You can achieve even more variety by masking lines to measure (see page 171).

BASIC RECIPE – MID AND DEEP BLUE ON TURQUOISE

MATERIALS

Quantities for Gingham Trunk (see page 115)
Base coats ▶ 400ml white vinyl matt emulsion / 100ml cerulean blue artists' acrylic colour (2 coats)
Rolling the grid ▶ 285ml white vinyl matt emulsion / 215ml ultramarine blue artists' acrylic colour

EQUIPMENT

3 containers for mixing paint / mixing sticks / 1 x 50mm (2in) emulsion brush / Chinagraph pencil or soft colour pencils (to match stripes) / ruler or straight edge / set square / 2 large plates / 2 x 25mm (1in) foam seam rollers / spare piece of board

METHOD
Base coats

1 Pour the emulsion into one of the containers, add the colour and stir well.
2 Apply two good, even coats to the primed and prepared surface (see pages 12–17) with the emulsion brush, allowing 2–3 hours for each coat to dry.

Planning

Using the Chinagraph (or colour) pencil, ruler (or straight edge) and set square, measure and draw a series of vertical and horizontal lines to create a grid of approx. 9cm (3½in) squares on the painted surface. If you are working on a piece with drawers, replace them first so the tartan on them will correspond to the overall pattern. Remove before painting!

Rolling the grid

1 Mix the mid blue in the second container, using 160ml white and 90ml (6tsbp) ultramarine blue and stirring well.
2 Pour a little at a time onto one of the large plates and flatten with the roller. Cover evenly by pushing the roller steadily through the paint and test on a piece of board.
3 Centre on one of the vertical grid lines and roll the paint onto the surface. Reload and, following the grid, roll in the remaining verticals. Allow to dry (1–2 hours).
4 Mix the deep blue, using the rest of the white and blue, and roll in the horizontals. Allow to dry (1–2 hours).

Notes If planning your own project, protect with a sealant for a hardwearing finish (see pages 42–3).

❶ TWO BLUES ON TURQUOISE
The basic recipe: you need to vary pressure and paint quantity to create the crossover look of gingham fabric. Experiment on a spare board first.

❷ RED GINGHAM
This classic colourway is very simply achieved, using the same premixed bright red emulsion (500ml) for verticals and horizontals on a base coat of 500ml white emulsion.

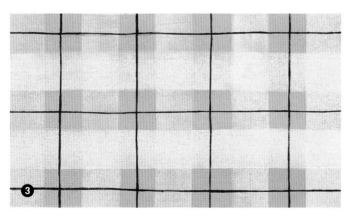

❸ SUNNY TARTAN
Base coat: 600ml white emulsion; artists' acrylics – 100ml bright green, 3⅓tbsp cadmium yellow. 1st grid: 300ml white emulsion; artists' acrylic – 3⅓tbsp pale olive green. 2nd grid: 2tbsp white emulsion; artists' acrylic – 4tbsp cadmium scarlet.

❹ TRAD TARTAN
Base coat: 500ml blue emulsion. 1st grid: 500ml emerald green emulsion. 2nd and 3rd grids: 6tbsps bright red emulsion and white emulsion. Liner 1 follows the 1st grid; liner 2 makes another by bisecting the 1st.

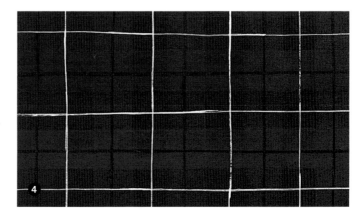

STAMPING

Like stencilling, stamped motifs are an excellent way to decorate a flat painted surface – wood, laminate or fabric. In their simplest form they can be improvised, like the chic spot design featured on the Stamped Café Table. Try cutting others from the cheapest sort of even-textured household sponge. Shop-bought stamps will give a hard-edged, accurate image and are now available in hundreds of designs. Or you can draw your own motifs and ask your local artshop for details of printers or specialist companies who will make them up for you.

BASIC RECIPE – USING ARTISTS' ACRYLICS OR EMULSION

MATERIALS

Quantities for Stamped Café Table – outer circle (see page 86) Stamping the spots ▶ 4tbsp titanium white artists' acrylic colour / 4tbsp permanent light blue (phthalocyanine blue) artists' acrylic colour

EQUIPMENT

2 saucers / mixing sticks / 2 x 35mm (1⅜in) diameter sponges for mini-roller

METHOD
Stamping the spots

1 Place the first colour (titanium white) on one of the saucers and use a mixing stick to flatten the paint slightly.
2 Dip the end of one of the dry sponge rollers into the paint and rock it gently from side to side, making sure it is completely covered. Now experiment with your simple stamp on a piece of board, pressing the end onto the surface to make a series of spots. You'll soon find out how much paint and pressure to apply.

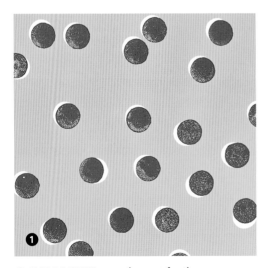

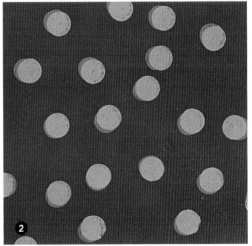

❶ **BLUE ON WHITE** Stamped on a plain yellow emulsion base (300ml), the basic recipe also suggests another colourway for the blind on page 61. This design could be adapted for fabric painting (see page 170).

❷ **PINK ON ORANGE** Base: 150ml white emulsion; artists' acrylics – 100ml crimson, 3½tbsp cadmium red. 1st stamp: artists' acrylic– 4tbsp cadmium red. 2nd stamp: artists' acrylics – 2½tbsp permanent rose, 1½tbsp titanium white.

3 Once you feel confident, reload the roller and stamp random spots all over the painted surface. Allow to dry (1 hour).

4 Using the same method and the second sponge roller, stamp the second colour on top of the first, positioning it slightly off centre. You are aiming for a blue spot with a just perceptible white highlight and the effect will be three dimensional. Allow to dry (1 hour).

Notes If planning your own project, protect with a sealant for a hardwearing finish (see pages 42–3).

USING INK STAMP PADS

The water-based ink stamp pads made for fabric printing are now available in a wide variety of colours and offer the best coverage, shortest drying-time and a good hardwearing finish for stamping on wood. The simple technique is the same for both surfaces. Push your bought stamp gently but firmly onto the pad, rocking it slightly to ensure complete coverage. Turn over to check and then press carefully down onto a test piece. Apply and remove equally carefully. Allow to dry (30 minutes).

I used a burgundy fabric stamp pad for the leaf and feather motifs on what had started life as an unpainted but sealed child's play table. The surface was prepared and primed (see pages 12–17) and then painted with a mix of 200ml white emulsion, 2tbsp yellow ochre and 4tsp raw umber (both artists' acrylics). The fabric lampshade was also stamped on a sponged base of 100ml acrylic scumble glaze, plus 5tsp dioxazine purple (see page 170, Glaze coat only, for the technique).

METAL EFFECTS

The interest in metal finishes on furniture shows no sign of abating. Ideas pages 92–3 give you some idea why. These are strong, dramatic effects with the potential to dominate modern or traditional settings – and they cost a fraction of the real thing! My pewter and copper finishes use a metallic spray for the base coat and recent improvements in quality mean that authenticity is now more easily attainable, but it's careful work at the glaze stage that produces results. Study the real thing if you can before creating the patination. Of course, verdigris – natural weathering on copper and bronze – is the ultimate aged metal effect. My verdigris relies on hand painting, but again look and learn from actual examples. Because bronze especially was often highly wrought for decorative effect, verdigris is also suited to areas of detail.

BASIC RECIPE – PEWTER

MATERIALS

Quantities for Moorish Quarter-Tester (see page 122)
Base coat ▶ 100ml silver spray paint
Glaze coat ▶ 150ml acrylic scumble glaze (transparent) / 2tbsp payne's grey artists' acrylic colour / 2tsp mars black artists' acrylic colour

EQUIPMENT

Dustsheets / protective mask / container for mixing glaze / large plate / 1 x 15mm (½in) round hoghair brush

METHOD
Base coat

PROTECT YOUR WORK SPACE WITH DUSTSHEETS BEFORE SPRAYING, WORK IN A WELL-VENTILATED AREA AND WEAR A MASK.

Shake the spray can well and apply an even coat to the prepared and primed surface (see pages 12–17), holding the can approx. 30.5cm (12in) from the surface and using steady, sweeping stokes. Allow to dry (1 hour).

Glaze coat

1 Pour the scumble glaze into the container. Add the payne's grey and mars black, stirring well.
2 Pouring a little of the glaze at a time onto the large plate, dip the tip of the hoghair brush into the glaze and dab it onto the surface. Apply lightly in some places, more heavily in others. The plate helps prevent brush overload.
3 Use the same brush to go quickly over the painted surface, stippling or very gently dabbing to take off a little of the glaze. Move your wrist rather than your arm and work randomly to create the 'dirty', mottled look of the aged metal – the glaze should still be heavier in some places than in others. Allow to dry (2–3 hours).

Notes If planning your own project, protect with a sealant for a hardwearing finish (see pages 42–3).

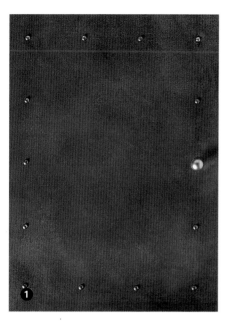

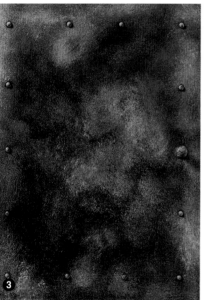

❶ PEWTER
Like copper, this adaptable finish works particularly well in kitchens.

❸ VERDIGRIS
Modify the Pewter Recipe as explained below. Base coats: 250ml blackboard paint (2 coats). Glaze colour-mix: artists' acrylics – 2½tbsp monestial green, 2½tbsp titanium white.

❷ COPPER
You can create a convincing aged copper effect by substituting the following colours in the Pewter Recipe. Base coat: copper spray paint. Glaze coat colour-mix: artists' acrylics – 3tbsp mars black, 2tsp burnt umber.

BASIC RECIPE – VERDIGRIS

There are two essential differences from the Pewter Recipe. First, the base is painted, not sprayed. Using a household brush, apply two coats of well-stirred blackboard paint to your prepared and primed surface (see pages 12–17, but remember there's no need to prime wood), allowing 3–4 hours for each coat to dry. Second, once the glaze has been stippled and before it dries, go over it again with the same brush, distributing the glaze as far as possible to reproduce the 'crusty' patination. See above for the glaze colour-mix.

GILDING

Gilding is best kept for decorative flourishes – on moulding or finials, for example – although it can claim centre stage (see the Gilded Table on page 75). Liquid leaf is the easiest to apply and quality is now high. Dutch metal leaf is cheaper and the effect is good but it is more time-consuming. Bronzing powders give a slightly frosted look and again take time. See page 35 for more about materials. Whichever method you use, I reckon ageing adds authenticity.

BASIC RECIPE – AGED GILDING USING METAL LEAF

MATERIALS

Quantities for Gilded Table (see page 75)
Base coat ▶ 350ml premixed deep blue vinyl matt emulsion
Size coat ▶ 350ml italian water-based size
Gilding ▶ 40 loose sheets gold dutch metal leaf
Sealant coat ▶ 3 tbsp transparent polish (clear)

EQUIPMENT

Mixing sticks / 1 x 50mm (2in) emulsion brush / 1 x 25mm (1in) flat bristle brush / disposable gloves / soft-bristled brush (optional) / clean dusters / lint-free cotton rags (optional)

METHOD
Base coat

Stir well and apply to the prepared and primed surface (see pages 12–17) with the emulsion brush. Allow to dry (2–3 hours).

Size coat

Again stirring well, apply a thin, even coat to the surface with the flat bristle brush. The more bubbles on the surface, the more uneven your size coat will be so don't overload your brush. Leave to become clear and tacky (15–20 minutes).

Gilding

1 Arrange your work space, placing the metal leaf close at hand.
2 Wearing the disposable gloves, carefully lift each leaf and lay it on the surface. Your aim is to cover most of the base coat, allowing a little to show through where natural ageing might occur – on raised details and at edges and corners, for example.
3 Smooth the surface carefully with the soft-bristled brush or clean duster (see page 35), working leaf gently into crevices and detail, and remove any excess leaf.

Sealant coat

Using a clean duster, rub the polish carefully onto the gilded surface with a circular motion. Allow to set (15 minutes) and very, very gently buff up with another clean duster.

Notes You can distress for further ageing before or after sealing by rubbing carefully with wirewool and methylated spirits. Allow to dry (1 hour). Or create ageing glazes tinted with acrylic colour to complement the base coat and middle grey to darken (see caption 2). Brush on after sealing; remove excess with cotton rag.

❶ LIGHT AGEING WITH METAL LEAF
Ageing is limited to the fine lines circling the finial. Dark base coats work well.

❷ HEAVY AGEING WITH METAL LEAF
Base: 320ml white emulsion; artists' acrylic – 2tbsp burnt umber. I used fragments of leaf and, after sealing, distressed the surface with wirewool and methylated spirits. Finally I added an ageing glaze, made of 1tsp acrylic scumble and artists' acrylics (1tsp cadmium red and ½tsp middle grey).

❸ LIQUID LEAF
No size is required; paint straight onto the base coat – I used 4⅔tbsp gold liquid leaf – and sand to age. Base: 260ml white emulsion; artists' acrylics – 4tbsp raw umber, 2tbsp cadmium red.

❹ BRONZE POWDERS
10g (⅓oz) copper bronze powders created this aged effect. See method below. Base coat: 290ml white emulsion; artists' acrylic – 4tbsp emerald green.

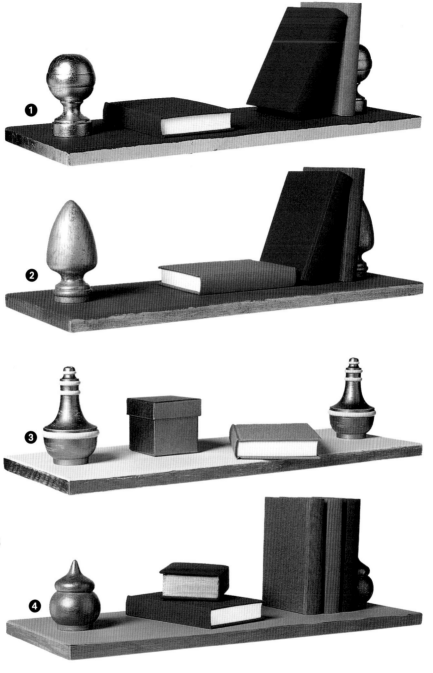

VARIATION – USING BRONZE POWDERS

ALWAYS WEAR A MASK AND WORK IN A WELL-VENTILATED AREA.

Choose a complementary base colour and apply the size coat as opposite. Using a flat artists' brush and taking up a little powder at a time, brush sparingly and gently onto the surface. Reload and repeat until the base coat is almost covered, imitating the effects of ageing. Carefully remove excess powder with the soft-bristled brush and apply the sealant with a household brush.

FABRIC PAINTING

① WARM YELLOW GRID ON MID BLUE
The basic recipe colourway: a lively and adaptable fifties retro look.

② SKY BLUE GRID ON PALE PINK
For this softer version, the glaze was tinted with 2½tbsp permanent rose and 1tbsp titanium white (both artists' acrylic colours). Two shades of aqua and a cerise fabric paint were used for the simple decoration.

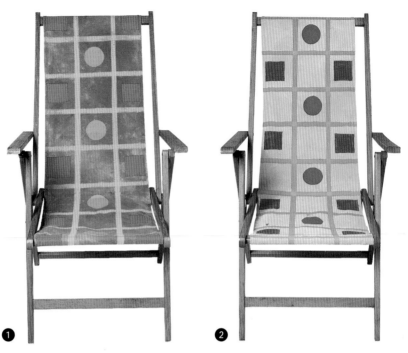

Personalized fabrics are a fun way to bring originality to classics like the deckchair or director's chair. Fabric paints and pens are easy to use and available in an increasing colour range to give instant results. By combining them with acrylic scumble and emulsions or artists' acrylics, I've created glazes for plain canvas which add enormously to their versatility. But remember strong colours are more fugitive in sunlight.

BASIC RECIPE – WARM YELLOW GRID ON MID BLUE

MATERIALS

Quantities for Deckchair (see above)
Glaze coat ▶ 150ml acrylic scumble glaze (transparent) / 2tbsp cobalt blue artists' acrylic colour / 1½tbsp titanium white artists' acrylic colour / 11oz artists' duck canvas (122 x 40cm/48 x 15¾in – see comment on fabric width below)
Decoration ▶ 150ml yellow fabric paint / 100ml peppermint green fabric paint / 100ml orange fabric paint

EQUIPMENT

Container for mixing glaze / mixing stick / sea sponge / water to dampen and rinse sponge / saucer / ruler or straight edge / pencil / set square / masking tape / lint-free cotton rags / 3 x 15mm (½in) round fitches / compass / coloured pencils (optional) / iron

METHOD
Glaze coat

1 Pour the acrylic scumble into the container, add the colours and stir well.
2 Soak the sponge in water and wring thoroughly. Pouring a little glaze onto the saucer, dip the sponge and apply to the fabric with a circular action. Repeat, aiming for a cloudy effect rather than blocks of colour. Allow to dry (1–2 hours).

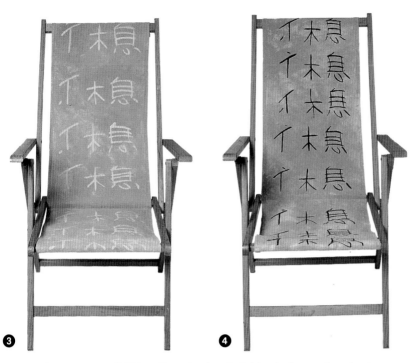

❸ JAPAN PURPLE
The acrylic colours in this pale glaze were 2tbsp dioxazine purple and 4tsp titanium white. I sketched the characters in pencil, applying lime fabric paint with a small fitch. They mean rest. See page 186 for reference.

❹ JAPAN GREY
Simpler still, here the glaze colour-mix is 2½tbsp middle grey and 1tbsp titanium white; black fabric paint for the characters.

Decoration

1 Using the ruler (or straight edge), pencil and set square, draw a series of evenly spaced vertical and horizontal lines on the fabric panel to create a grid of squares. Our deck chairs were narrower than the standard size and so was the canvas; my grid was based on a 13.5cm (5¼in) square.

2 Removing some of the tack on clean rags, stick a strip of masking tape on either side of each vertical line to create stripes approx. 12mm (½in) wide.

3 Paint in the vertical stripes with fabric paint, using one of the fitches and brushing away from the tape to prevent the paint 'bleeding' under it. Remove the tape carefully and allow to dry (1 hour).

4 Create a series of horizontal stripes of the same size and colour, using the same method.

5 With the compass and pencil draw a vertical row of circles in alternate squares down the middle of the fabric panel.

6 Use the second fitch and second fabric colour to fill in the circles, carefully concealing the pencil outlines. If a steady hand is not yours to command, it's worth drawing the circles and later the squares with appropriate coloured pencils. Allow to dry (1 hour).

7 Working from top to bottom, draw a freehand square in the two outer squares of each empty row so that the pairs of squares and single circles alternate.

8 Using the third fitch and third fabric colour, fill in the squares, again concealing the outlines. Allow to dry (1 hour).

9 Carefully press the reverse of the fabric with a medium-hot iron to seal the paint.

RUSH DYEING

Dyeing rush or basket weave is one of the lesser-known battery of options. But good colour and a sound finish are easily attainable so it's certainly a possibility if deciding the fate of tired old garden-room furniture. I've opted for strong tones with maximum impact but pastels can be equally successful. Unfinished rush or basket weave is the ideal base but rare. Don't despair – you'll find all the advice you'll need for working on sealed or prepainted surfaces on pages 12–13 and 16–17. See also the warning about loom chairs on page 106.

BASIC RECIPE – BRIGHT RED

MATERIALS

Quantities for Laundry Basket (see opposite)
Glaze coat ▶ 125ml acrylic scumble glaze (transparent) / 325ml deep cadmium red artists' acrylic colour

EQUIPMENT

Container for mixing glaze / mixing stick / 1 x 75mm (3in) household brush / lint-free cotton rags

METHOD
Glaze coat

1 Pour the acrylic scumble into the container, add the acrylic colour and stir well.
2 Brushing in the direction of the weave or rushes, apply the glaze to the entire surface. Take care to work it thoroughly into all the nooks and crannies.
3 With a series of clean rags folded into pads, go quickly over the surface, taking off any excess glaze and again working in the direction of the weave or rush. Allow to dry (3–4 hours).

Notes If planning your own project, protect with a sealant for a hardwearing finish (see pages 42–3).

MAKING THE LAUNDRY BAG

Size and shape requirements will vary. For my basket – approx. 51cm (20in) tall with a diameter of 56cm (22in) – I used cotton measuring 1.5m x 140cm (5ft x 56in). Whatever the size, the method is the same. You need three newspaper templates: one for the base, one long piece for the sides and one rectangular piece of the same length for the gathered, upper section. Measure and cut to fit, adding 15mm (⅝in) allowances all round for turnings plus another 5cm (2in) at the top for the drawstring casing. If your basket is flared, the side template will need flared ends. Check the templates for fit before cutting. Machine sew the upper section to the side and then from top to bottom before attaching the base and making the open-ended casing. Thread with cord.

❶ BRIGHT RED
The colourway of the basic recipe: like all the other baskets, it was finally sealed with 125ml acrylic varnishing wax.

❷ YELLOW
I substituted 325ml cadmium yellow artists' acrylic colour in the glaze coat to produce this deep, warm tone.

❸ DEEP BLUE
Here I used 325ml ultramarine artists' acrylic. Reserve it for small projects because this colour is one of the most expensive.

❹ PURPLE
Dioxazine purple in the standard quantity tinted the basket weave. All four baskets had to be sanded before glazing.

MOSAIC

Mosaic is a great way to makeover flat surfaces. With colours as sober or colourful as you like you can create designs of startling complexity or, as I prefer, total simplicity. There's a vast range of experience to inspire you, either high historical, in the work of the craftsmen of Rome, Islam, Byzantium or the Italian Renaissance, or in the folk traditions that popularized those amazing skills. My designs rely for their effect on bright colour, the combination of whole and broken tiles, and tinted grouts which produce a softly aged look as the wash sits in the crazing. I love my Café Table (see page 85) but these little doors please me too because they open up possibilities for transforming vertical surfaces.

BASIC RECIPE – APPLE MOTIF

MATERIALS

Quantities for Apple Door (58.5 x 58.5cm/23 x 23in)
Preparation ▶ approx. 160 red tiles / 80 pale to mid green tiles / 30 orange tiles / 20 dark green tiles
Fixing the tiles ▶ 150ml high-bond PVA adhesive and sealer or 200g (7oz) ceramic tile adhesive
Grouting the tiles ▶ 150ml ready-mixed white ceramic grout
Tinting the grout ▶ 2tsp yellow artists' acrylic colour / 3½tsp water

EQUIPMENT

Metal rule / A2 layout paper / ruler or straight edge / pencil / spare piece of chipboard (to required size – see below) / photocopier / scissors / warm soapy water and towel (if required – see below) / 1 x 15mm (½in) round fitch (for PVA) or spatula (for ceramic adhesive) / tile nippers / protective glasses / box to catch pieces / old sheet / rubber mallet / mixing sticks / grout spreader or filler knife / household sponge / water to dampen sponge / saucer / 1 x 25mm (1in) household brush / lint-free cotton rags

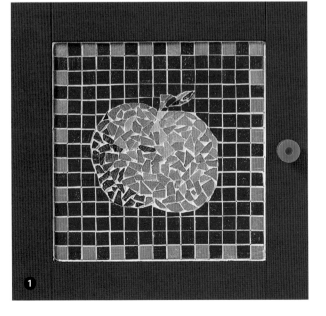

❶ APPLE MOTIF
Add a total of 300ml deep blue emulsion (2 coats) for the frame and you have a terrific update for a simple panel door in a kitchen or bathroom. I smashed the tiles in a folded sheet to create the irregular shapes in the motif.

METHOD
Preparation

1 Draw a scale plan on layout paper of the area you wish to decorate, using the metal rule, ruler (or straight edge) and pencil, and secure to a spare piece of chipboard.

2 Enlarge the motif (see page 187) to the required size, using a photocopier. Cut out and use as a template to draw the basic outline on your plan. Set the template aside for later use.

3 Check the approximate positions of the background tiles. If you bought them mounted on backing paper, soak in warm, soapy water and wipe dry with a towel. Work from the outside inwards, allowing for the grout between them. The standard spacing is approx. 1mm (½₂in) and that's the spacing adopted on the mounted squares of 15 x 15 in which they are sometimes sold. The size or style of a design may require a different allowance but it is best to keep it uniform. Don't trim tiles, even where the design is to feature broken pieces. Just note where trimming will be necessary. For complex designs I like to keep this rough layout, transferring the tiles as required.

4 Using the template again, draw the basic outline of the motif on the prepared surface (see pages 12–17). This is the time to make small adjustments to its size, if necessary. There is no need to prime under the tiles when working on wood.

Fixing the tiles

1 If using PVA adhesive and the fitch, apply an even coat to part of the edge of the design – enough for approx. eight tiles. Lay the edge tiles, working from corners if there are any. Use the ruler to keep rows straight. You can, if you prefer, brush the adhesive onto the back of each tile and position (see page 41). If using ceramic adhesive, adopt the same method, bedding the tiles into an even layer of adhesive spread with the spatula.

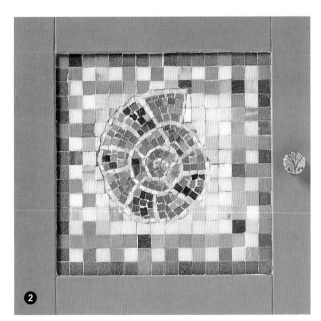

❷ AMMONITE
The regular shapes needed for the fossil were cut with tile nippers. The grout was tinted with 2tsp pale blue artists' acrylic; the colour-mix for the two lilac coats on the frame was 250ml white emulsion and 3½tbsp dioxazine purple artists' acrylic. See page 187 for the motif.

175

2 Continue in the same way, working inwards and on small areas at a time, until you have laid the whole background tiles.

3 Using the nippers, trim the remaining background tiles to fit around the motif. Cut with the reverse (ridged) side of the tile facing upwards (see page 41). You'll need to press hard and suddenly. Wear protective glasses and work over a box – that way you save small pieces which could be useful for broken-tile sections and prevent shards of glass falling to the floor.

4 Glue (or bed) the trimmed pieces in position around the motif to complete the background.

5 To create the broken pieces within the motif, use the tile nippers as described above or, for a more random effect, place tiles of the required colour on part of a folded sheet, fold it in half again to cover the tiles, and (wearing the protective glasses) tap them sharply with the mallet.

6 Working on areas of detail (such as the shading, leaf and stalk) first, glue (or bed) the broken pieces into place. All your jigsaw puzzle skills are useful here. But remember there is no right way to lay these areas: you are aiming first for an effect which pleases you and second (as far as possible) for uniform spacing between the tiles.

Grouting the tiles

1 Stir the tile grout well and apply to the tiled surface with the spreader (or filler knife), pushing grout firmly into the spaces between the tiles.

2 Remove any excess with the spreader and replace it in the tub. You can use it again.

3 Immerse the sponge in water, wring out until just damp and carefully wipe the tiles clean. Allow to dry (8 hours).

Tinting the grout

1 Place the acrylic colour on a saucer, add the water and stir well until the wash is the consistency of single cream.

2 Apply to the entire surface, using the household brush.

3 Working quickly with a damp rag, wipe off the excess. Allow to dry (1–2 hours) and buff up with a clean rag.

Notes Prime the surrounding surfaces before you tile but leave the rest of the painting until the mosaic is completed. You'll need to use masking tape to protect tiled areas. Take some of the tack off on a cloth first or you may disturb the grout when you remove the tape.

Remember, if planning a similar project, that tiles in quantity are heavy and can strain the door hinges. Stronger hinges may be the answer but don't create whole panels of mosaic on large doors. One solution on a solid wooden door is to opt for borders or bands of mosaic set into routed sections.

PUNCHED TIN

Unlike mosaic, punched tin is best kept for vertical surfaces, although I can see it working on a tiny decorative table or, on a larger scale, on something like a blanket box. It needs plain, uncluttered shapes too and not just because of the practical difficulties of applying tin to curved or rounded furniture. Pennsylvania German tradition is the current inspiration for this wonderfully easy technique. These people favoured symmetrical designs like snowflakes, tulips and hearts. Here and on the French Dresser (page 70) I've kept my motifs simple and formal, based largely on straight and curved lines, though the references are sophisticated. If you want to try for something more complex, there is an earlier European tradition which favoured intricate patterns and I have seen illustrations of elaborate, fifteenth-century lanterns used to guide travellers to taverns deep in the Vienna Woods. I'd like to experiment with the tree of life motif that crops up in all Indo-European cultures. The traditional material was coke tin – pure tin was too soft and expensive for what has always been a folk art. Today tin-plated steel is the standard but zinc is an acceptable substitute. Both need to be rubbed down with wet and dry paper for an authentic look.

BASIC RECIPE – TOPIARY MOTIFS

MATERIALS

Quantities for Four-Panelled Door (see page 178)
Preparation ▶ tin-plated steel sheet or zinc (see below)
Finishing ▶ 100ml paint thinners / 100ml beeswax polish
Securing the tin ▶ 100ml strong-bonding, multi-purpose contact adhesive / brass or copper-headed nails (see pages 178 and 179)

EQUIPMENT

Metal rule / ruler or straight edge / pencil / newspaper for template (if required – see below) / scissors / masking tape / Chinagraph pencil / tin snips / rubber or wooden mallet / large sheet chipboard (to required size – see page 179) / photocopier / A2 tracing paper / centre or nail punch / hammer / cotton gloves / wet and dry paper / lint-free cotton rags / 1 round fitch / bradawl

METHOD
Preparing the tin

1 Measure and cut out the appropriate template(s) for your chosen panels on newspaper, using the metal rule, ruler (or straight edge) and pencil. For our door we needed four rectangles – two 89 x 19cm (35 x 7½in) and two 45.75 x 19cm (18 x 7½in) – which we drew straight onto the metal, but templates are often helpful when working on more complicated shapes.

2 Secure the template(s) on the metal sheet with masking tape and use the Chinagraph pencil to draw the outlines.

PUNCHED TIN

Life less ordinary for a flush door: for the motifs, see page 187. Note the variation on the upper panels: I punched on either side of the line when creating the pots. Once the metal panels had been stuck into position, we added already primed strips of simple pine trim to create four fake door panels, securing it with small copper-headed nails. The prepared and primed door frame was given two base coats of pale green emulsion (totalling 500ml), dry brushed with a glaze-mix of 100ml acrylic scumble glaze and 250ml deep moss green emulsion and allowed to dry for 2–3 hours. Finally, it was sealed with two coats of matt acrylic varnish. We used zinc instead of tin for this project. To compare the look of tin-plated steel, see page 70.

3 Using the tin snips, cut out the panel(s), and then flatten the raised, cut edges by tapping them gently with the rubber (or wooden) mallet.

4 After positioning the panel(s) to check for fit and trimming and flattening where necessary, cover the edges with masking tape to prevent cuts and grazes.

5 Secure the panel(s) to the chipboard, using masking tape across the corners.

6 Using a photocopier, enlarge your chosen motif(s) (see page 187) to the required size.

7 Transfer to the tracing paper and, again using masking tape, position the tracing(s) on the panel(s).

Punching the tin

1 Working from left to right (if right-handed) and top to bottom, place the centre (or nail) punch over one of the lines and strike it gently with the hammer (see page 40). You are aiming to make a clear indentation – not to pierce the metal.

2 Reposition the punch 1–2cm (⅜–¾in) below the first hole on the same line and repeat the action. Continue until you have punched in all the lines of the motif(s).

3 Using the same method, punch in the 'freehand' holes – the ones within the triangle and circle which form the topiary shapes. It's up to you how you do this – rule guide lines for a neat, formal effect or create a more spontaneous look with random indentations. Remove the tracing(s).

Finishing

1 Put on the cotton gloves and wear them for the whole of this stage to avoid getting fingerprints on the metal.

2 Turn the metal over and, using the mallet, hammer the dents out gently. This won't affect the look of the design – you are simply flattening the reverse side(s) so that the metal will adhere better when glued.

3 Turn back to the right side and rub with wet and dry paper, using a gentle, circular action to create that characteristic rubbed-down look of finished tin.

4 Clean with paint thinners, applied with pads of folded rag.

5 Again using clean rags, quickly rub on a thin, even coat of beeswax polish, leave to set (15 minutes) and buff up with another clean rag.

Securing the tin

1 Following the manufacturer's instructions, use the fitch to apply even coats of contact adhesive onto both the panel(s) and the wood, position and leave to set.

2 For panelled doors, tap a brass nail gently into all four corners of each panel for added security, preparing the pilot holes with a bradawl. For fake panels, see caption opposite.

FROSTED GLASS

For years the designs available in commercial frosted glass were limited and uninspiring, and it is not surprising that such glass was mostly to be found where privacy was the overriding principle. Manufacturers are now producing more imaginative patterns and etched glass alternatives, but they are frequently expensive, and the frosting method described here demonstates just how easy it is to produce inexpensive frosted effects for yourself. You can colour the water-based frosting varnish with special colourizers, and this adds enormously to the versatility of the technique, making it one that you will certainly want to use beyond the bathroom. It is, unfortunately, not easy to maintain consistency over large areas so choose simple designs on small projects.

BASIC RECIPE – LEAF MOTIF

MATERIALS

Quantity for Small Door (32 x 36cm/12½ x 14in)
Frosting ▶ 5tsp frosting varnish

EQUIPMENT

25mm (1in) masking tape (for fitted glass) or gaffer tape (for unfitted glass) / scissors / window cleaner / lint-free cotton rags / photocopier / pencil / 1 sheet A4 self-adhesive matt clear transfer film / scalpel / cutting mat / large plate / 1 x 25mm (1in) household brush / 1 x 100mm (4in) sponge mini-roller

METHOD
Preparing the glass

1 If the glass is already fitted in the door frame, cover the retaining battens or putty with masking tape to protect them. If working with unfitted glass, cover the edges with strips of gaffer tape to avoid injury.
2 Using window cleaner and clean rag, wipe the glass carefully, taking care not to dampen the tape. Use another clean rag to dry the glass. It must be dust and fingerprint free.

Masking

1 Enlarge the motif on page 187 to size, using a photocopier.
2 Trace the motif onto the self-adhesive film with the pencil and carefully cut round the outline of the leaf and its 'skeleton', using the scalpel and cutting mat.
3 Peel the backing off the film motif (now without its skeleton) and position on the glass, taking care not to mark it.

Frosting

1 Pour frosting varnish onto the large plate and apply a thin, even coat to the entire surface, using the household brush.
2 Working quickly and lightly in all directions, go over the wet surface with the dry sponge roller. Your aim is to get rid of the brush marks so that no lines remain on the surface.
3 Using the tip of the scalpel, remove the motif and any masking tape quickly and carefully before the varnish begins to dry or you may lift some of the frosting off with it. Allow to dry (2–4 hours).

❶ LEAF MOTIF
The basic recipe: the leaf-shaped mask creates the design.

❷ CACTUS
Here the method is reversed. The film surrounding the cut motif protects most of the glass so it must be large enough to cover the whole panel. Add 1tsp green colourizer before application and mix well. See page 187 for motif.

❸ CHEQUERS
To achieve this effect rule a grid of 5cm (2in) squares on A3 tracing paper and lay it under the glass as a guide. Mask alternate squares by applying 5 x 5cm (2 x 2in) pieces of film to the glass before frosting.

❹ FISHES
Follow the method for example 2, but substitute 1tsp blue colourizer. See page 187 for the motif.

DESIGNING MOTIFS

I used self-adhesive matt clear transfer film for all the designs illustrated above and for the coffee-cup design used on the French Dresser (see page 70). It makes good contact with the glass and therefore prevents the frosting from spreading where it is not wanted. For more about the method, see page 31.

Simple, graphic designs work best, and remember that you can achieve either positive or negative effects. The fish illustrated above, for example, could be clear, while the rest of the glass is frosted. In fact, I prefer to frost most of the glass and leave the motif clear when working with figurative designs – the effect is always less cluttered.

Notes Use only soapy water to clean frosted glass.

MOTIFS AND TEMPLATES

Here are the motifs and templates used in our projects for you to adapt for your own makeovers. All of them can be enlarged very simply with a photocopier to a size to suit your particular piece. Check the scaled templates before cutting – you may need or want to adjust the shape. We hope you'll be inspired to mix and match the motifs too – the bee or leaf, for example, could make handsome mosaics.

VASE STENCILS
Place four small marks on each stencil as shown. Check they match exactly. Transfer to the painted surface once the basic shape is dry to align the second stencil (illustrated on page 39).

Page 58: Stencilled Set of Drawers

PATTERN FOR ZINC WORKTOP
Adapt this shape to suit your own project. Blue lines indicate cut lines; red lines show fold lines. Don't overlook the small cuts separating the the sides from the front and back.

Front

Pages 70–4: French Dresser

Backplate (not in proportion)

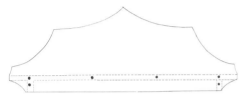

ATTACHING
THE BACKPLATE
Note the screw
positions. If your
table has no base,
attach a batten
underneath it.

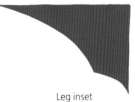

Leg inset

Pages 80–3: Console Tables

Pages 106–9: Loom Chairs

Page 116: Crustacean Mirror

Shelf base (not in proportion)

Shelf backplate

Pages 118–21: Decorated Headboard

Quarter-tester front (in proportion)

Tieback backplate (not in proportion)

Quarter-tester side (in proportion)

Pages 122–5: Moorish Quarter-Tester

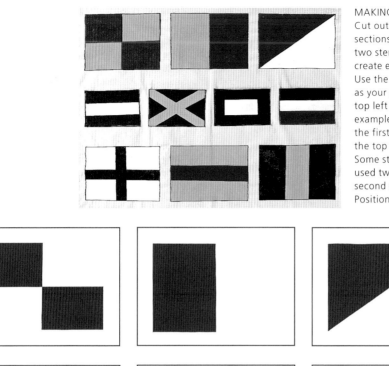

MAKING FLAGS
Cut out the blue sections. You need two stencils to create each flag. Use the illustration as your guide. The top left flag, for example, combines the first stencil in the top two rows. Some stencils are used twice for a second colourway. Position with care.

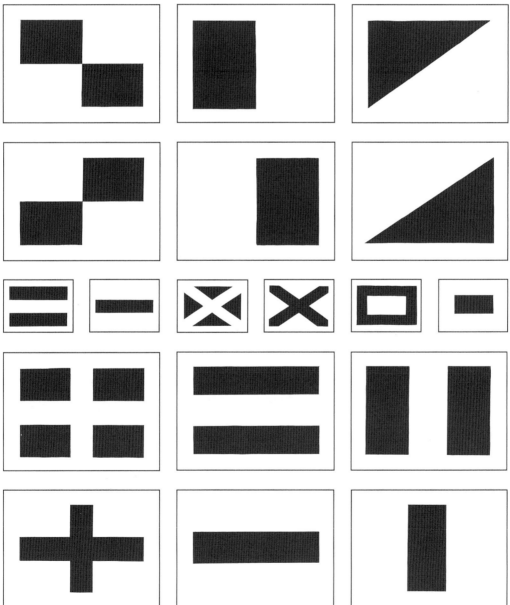

Pages 128–9: Nautical Banner

DAISY STENCILS
A two-part stencil plus mask: the method is clearly described in the technique. Just remember to cut the larger of the two circles out carefully and retain.

Pages 157–9: Stencilling

Pages 170–1: Fabric Painting

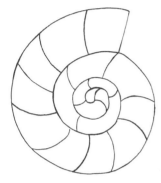

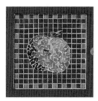

Pages 177–9: Punched Tin

Pages 174–6: Mosaic

Pages 180–1: Frosted Glass

LIST OF SUPPLIERS

Most of the materials and equipment described in this book can be found in your local artists' supplies shop, DIY warehouse, woodyard or builders' merchant. If you have any difficulty, consult the list below. A number of the companies listed here have mail-order facilities. However, some suppliers will not dispatch toxic or inflammable materials by post.

✉ Indicates that a mail-order service is available.

The Bead Shop
21a Tower Street
London WC2H 9NS
0171-240 0931
Supplier of beads, thread and wire

Bladerubber Stamps ✉
2 Neal's Yard
London WC2H 9DP
0171-379 7391
Supplier of rubber stamps, water-based ink pads and stencils

J.W. Bollom & J.T. Keep
P.O. Box 78
Croydon Road
Beckenham
Kent BR3 4BL
0181-658 2299
Manufacturer of brushes, crackle varnish, artists' colours and scumble glaze

Brodie and Middleton Ltd ✉
68 Drury Lane
London WC2B 5SP
0171-836 3289
Supplier of brushes, metallic powders and artists' colours

Cornelissen and Son Ltd ✉
105 Great Russell Street
London WC1B 3RY
0171-636 1045
Manufacturer and supplier of gilding materials and artists' colours

Daler-Rowney Ltd
12 Percy Street
London W1A 2BP
0171-636 8241
Manufacturer of wide range of standard artists' materials

Ells & Farrier ✉
20 Beak Street
London W1R 3HA
0171-629 9964
Supplier of beads, jewels and studs

The English Stamp Company ✉
Sunnydown
Worth Matravers
Dorset BHI9 3JP
01929 439117
Manufacturer of rubber stamps and paints with made-to-order service

Farrow and Ball
33 Uddens Trading Estate
Wimborne
Dorset BH21 7NL
01202 876141
Manufacturer of excellent range of historical paint colours, developed for The National Trust

Fired Earth plc ✉
Twyford Mill
Oxford Road
Adderbury
Oxfordshire OX17 3HP
01295 812088
Manufacturer of paints, including colours suitable for 19th-century interiors, and tiles and fabrics

Green and Stone ✉
259 King's Road
London SW3 5EL
0171-352 0837
Supplier of brushes, crackle varnish, artists' colours, scumble glaze and stencil card

Home Crafts Direct ✉
P.O. Box 38
Leicester LE1 9BU
0116 251 3139
Supplier of general arts and crafts supplies, including chrome trim and small tin sheets

Jali Ltd ✉
Aspley House
Chartham
Canterbury
Kent CT4 7HT
01227 831710
Supplier of decorative unpainted edge trims and fretwork panels

Leyland Paint
Kalon Decorative Products
Huddersfield Road
Birstall, Batley
West Yorkshire WF17 9XA
01924 477201
Manufacturer of paint, varnish, glaze and artists' colours. Stockists throughout the country

John Myland Ltd ✉
80 Norwood High Street
West Norwood
London SE27 9NW
0181-670 9161
Supplier of waxes, varnishes and wood finishes

Neal Street East
5 Neal Street
London WC2H 9PU
0171-240 0135
Supplier of shells and beads

Paint Library ✉
5 Elystan Street
London SW3 3NT
0171-823 7755
Supplier of high-quality, modern and historical paint colours and fabric paints

Paper and Paints
4 Park Walk
London SW10 0AD
0171-352 8626
Manufacturer of historical paints, with colour-matching service

E. Ploton (Sundries) Ltd ✉
273 Archway Road
London N6 5AA
0181-348 2838
Supplier of brushes, gilding materials and artists' colours

Polyvine
Vine House
Rockhampton, Berkeley
Gloucestershire GL13 9DT
01454 261276
Manufacturer of water-based products, including frosting varnish and scumble glaze

Russell & Chapple Ltd ✉
23 Monmouth Street
London WC2 9DE
0171-836 7521
Supplier of artists' canvas and general art supplies

Screwfix Direct ✉
Houndstone Business Park
Yeovil, Somerset BA22 8RT
0500 414141
Supplier of screws, fixings and tools

Stuart Stevenson
68 Clerkenwell Road
London EC1M 5QA
0171-253 1693
Supplier of gilding materials

BIBLIOGRAPHY

Bickman, George. *The Universal Penman*, Dover, New York, 1968.

Butsch, Albert Fidelis. *The Handbook of Renaissance Ornament*, Dover, New York, 1969.

Carter, David, and Heming, Charles. *'Homes and Gardens' Complete Paint Book*, Conran Octopus, London, 1996.

Colling, James Kellaway. *Medieval Decorative Ornament*, Dover, New York, 1995.

Deberny Type Foundry. *Advertising Cuts*, Dover, New York, 1991.

Hall, Dinah. *Ethnic by Design*, Mitchell Beazley, London, 1992.

Pugin, Augustus Charles. *Pugin's Gothic Ornament*, Dover, New York, 1987.

Stewart, Bill. *Signwork: A Craftsman's Manual*, Collins: BSP

INDEX

ACKNOWLEDGMENTS

AUTHORS' ACKNOWLEDGMENTS

There are so many people we need to thank for their help in the production of this book: Mary Evans, Jane O'Shea and Rachel Gibson at Quadrille; the valiant Mary Davies, our editor, who certainly now knows her single-slot from her cross-head; Netty, for all her hard work and patience in sometimes fraught situations; Kate, Dee, Paul, Simon and Debs, for stepping into the breach so admirably on many occasions; Debbie Patterson and Nicki Dowey for their wonderful photography, what magicians they are; Alf and Rob at Dimmock Bros.; and lastly our neighbours, who have frequently put up with us turning the communal garden into a workshop.

PICTURE ACKNOWLEDGMENTS

The publishers wish to thank the following photographers and organizations for their kind permission to reproduce the photographs in this book:

6 above Rodney Weidland / Belle / Arcaid; 6 below Dominic Blackmore / Ideal Home / Robert Harding Syndication; 7 Gilles de Chabaneix / stylist: C. de Chabaneix / Marie Claire Idées; 8 above Ray Main / cupboard from David Gill Gallery, London; 8 below Ray Main / contemporary textile artist: Lauren Shanley, Studio 4, Gabriel's Wharf, 56 Upper Ground, London SE1 9PP; 10–11 Geoffry Frosh / Homes and Gardens / Robert Harding Syndication; 46–7 Simon Brown / Interior Archive; 48 Trevor Richards / Homes and Gardens / Robert Harding Syndication; 49 above Henry Wilson / Interior Archive; 49 below Gilles de Chabaneix / stylist: C. de Chabaneix / Marie Claire Idées; 136–7 J.L. Scotto / Agence Top; 138 David Parmiter; 139 above Alexander van Berge / Ouders van Nu; 139 below Richard Bryant / Arcaid.

Special photography was by Debbie Patterson and studio photography by Nicki Dowey. The spray paint illustrations are by Clive Goodyer and all other illustrations are by Liz Wagstaff.

PROPERTY ACKNOWLEDGMENTS

The publishers also wish to thank the following companies, who kindly lent properties for special photography:

Damask, Mail Order Dept, 7 Sullivan Enterprise Centre, Sullivan Road, London SW6 3DJ, tel. 0171–731 3470; Rayment Wirework, The Forge, Minster, Kent, tel. 01843 821628; Millenium, 1b–1d, High Street, Barnes, London SW13 9LB, tel. 0181–878 3553, and 12 Abingdon Road, Kensington, London W8 6AF, tel. 0171–938 3456.